# THE MAPLE CROWN IN ALBERTA:
# THE OFFICE OF LIEUTENANT-GOVERNOR

## 1905-2005

© Copyright 2005 Kenneth Munro.
All rights reserved. No part of this publication may be reproduced, stored in a retrieval system, or transmitted, in any form or by any means, electronic, mechanical, photocopying, recording, or otherwise, without the written prior permission of the author.

Note for Librarians: a cataloguing record for this book that includes Dewey Decimal Classification and US Library of Congress numbers is available from the Library and Archives of Canada. The complete cataloguing record can be obtained from their online database at:
www.collectionscanada.ca/amicus/index-e.html
ISBN 1-4120-5317-x
Printed in Victoria, BC, Canada

*Printed on paper with minimum 30% recycled fibre. Trafford's print shop runs on "green energy" from solar, wind and other environmentally-friendly power sources.*

# TRAFFORD

*Offices in Canada, USA, Ireland and UK*

This book was published *on-demand* in cooperation with Trafford Publishing. On-demand publishing is a unique process and service of making a book available for retail sale to the public taking advantage of on-demand manufacturing and Internet marketing. On-demand publishing includes promotions, retail sales, manufacturing, order fulfilment, accounting and collecting royalties on behalf of the author.

**Book sales for North America and international:**
Trafford Publishing, 6E–2333 Government St.,
Victoria, BC v8t 4p4 CANADA
phone 250 383 6864 (toll-free 1 888 232 4444)
fax 250 383 6804; email to orders@trafford.com

**Book sales in Europe:**
Trafford Publishing (UK) Ltd., Enterprise House, Wistaston Road Business Centre,
Wistaston Road, Crewe, Cheshire cw2 7rp UNITED KINGDOM
phone 01270 251 396 (local rate 0845 230 9601)
facsimile 01270 254 983; orders.uk@trafford.com

**Order online at:**
trafford.com/05-0212

10  9  8  7  6  5  4  3  2

To His Honour, the late H.A. "Bud" Olson
and
Dr. Lorne Tyrrell, Professor and former Dean of Medicine
University of Alberta
*who made this book possible*

# The Maple Crown

## The Queen

(Photo courtesy of the office of the Secretary to the Governor General)

Her Majesty Queen Elizabeth II,
Queen of Canada

## The Governor General

(Photo courtesy of the office of the Secretary to the Governor General)

Her Excellency,
The Right Honourable Adrienne Clarkson

## The Lieutenant-Governor

(Photo courtesy of Larry Wong, Edmonton Journal)

His Honour,
The Honourable Norman Kwong

# TABLE OF CONTENTS

| | |
|---|---|
| ACKNOWLEDGMENTS | i |
| | iii |
| PREFACE | |

## I    THE MAPLE CROWN

| | |
|---|---|
| Constitutional Monarchy | 1 |
| The Monarch and Lieutenant-Governors | 20 |
|     Visit to the Sovereign | 20 |
|     The Crown Made Visible | 23 |
|     Correspondence | 24 |
| Governor General and Lieutenant-Governors | 25 |
| Aides-de-camp | 29 |
| Expenditure on Office of Lieutenant-Governor | 30 |

## II    THE SYMBOLS OF OFFICE    38

| | |
|---|---|
| Privy Seal of the Lieutenant-Governor | 38 |
| Vice-Regal Salute | 40 |
| Vice-Regal Gun Salutes | 40 |
| The Lieutenant-Governor's Flag | 42 |
| The Lieutenant-Governor's Badge of Office | 45 |
| Official Residence | 50 |
| Transportation | 70 |
| Chancellorship of the Order of Excellence | 75 |
| Vice-Prior of the Most Venerable Order of St. John of Jerusalem | 77 |
| University of Alberta Visitor and LLD Degrees | 81 |

## III    POWERS OF THE CROWN    93

| | |
|---|---|
| Continuity of government | 93 |
| The Lieutenant-Governor's relationship with the Premier | 99 |
| The Right to be Consulted, to Encourage and occasionally to Warn | 103 |
| Royal Assent | 110 |

| | |
|---|---|
| Appropriations for Public Spending | 113 |
| Proclamations and Orders-in-Council | 114 |
| Crown as Custodian of Powers of the State | 115 |

## IV  STATE CEREMONIAL                119

| | |
|---|---|
| Installation | 119 |
| Opening of the Legislature | 144 |
| Swearing in Premier and MLAs | 155 |
| Greeting Official Visitors | 158 |
| Unveiling of Official Portrait | 167 |
| State Funerals | 172 |
|     His Honour Philip Primrose | 173 |
|     His Honour John Bowlen | 175 |
|     His Honour Grant MacEwan | 176 |
|     Other Vice-regal Funerals | 178 |

## V  OFFICIAL PUBLIC YEARLY CALENDAR OF THE LIEUTENANT-GOVERNOR                187

| | |
|---|---|
| The New Year's Levee | 187 |
| Victoria Day | 200 |
| Canada Day | 204 |
| Remembrance Day | 205 |
|     The Poppy Campaign | 206 |
|     Annual Remembrance Day Service | 211 |
| Investitures and Award Ceremonies | 216 |
|     The Alberta Order of Excellence | 216 |
|     Queen's Counsel | 218 |
|     The Order of St. John of Jerusalem | 220 |
|     The Duke of Edinburgh Awards | 222 |
|     Other Award Ceremonies | 222 |
| Other Functions | 223 |
|     The Canadian Derby | 226 |
|     The Consular Ball | 227 |
| Lieutenant-Governor Trophy (The Bulyea Cup) | 228 |
| Other Ceremonies | 232 |

| VI | CONCLUSION | 245 |
| VII | POSTSCRIPT | 249 |

APPENDICES                                              255

Installation
Visit to Sovereign
Honourary Degree from the University of Alberta
Investiture into the Order of St. John of Jerusalem
Portrait Unveiling
Deaths and State Funerals
Royal Visits to Alberta since 1951

BIBLIOGRAPHY                                            265

INDEX                                                   273

## ACKNOWLEDGMENTS

In preparing *The Maple Crown in Alberta: The Office of Lieutenant-Governor*, I have benefitted from the advice and suggestions of many individuals who are knowledgeable about the Crown in Canada. John Aimers, President of The Monarchist League of Canada, Brian Hodgson, Sergeant-at-Arms of the Alberta Legislative Assembly, and Blake McDougall, the former Legislature Librarian read earlier drafts of the manuscript and made helpful criticisms. I also wish to thank the Office of Her Excellency Adrienne Clarkson for photographs and Mary Hunt in the Office of the Lieutenant-Governor of Alberta for providing information about the Office. In addition, the staff at the Legislature Library, the City of Edmonton Archives and the Provincial Archives were most helpful. In particular, I wish to thank Betty Anne Spinks, Chief of Protocol for the Province of Alberta and Sherry Bell of the Legislative Library.

The Faculty of Arts at the University of Alberta provided me with two SAS grants which allowed me to hire a student to carry out research in specific areas related to activities of various Lieutenant-Governors. I wish to thank Darlene Dugbazah specifically for her uncovering valued information. In addition, staff at the University of Alberta Library, Archives, Bruce Peel Special Collections Library and the Photography Services of Client Services, before it was disbanded, were all most helpful. I also wish to thank the Speaker of the Legislative Assembly of Alberta, the Honourable Ken Kowalski, Canadian Press, Associated Press, The *Edmonton Journal* library, the *Edmonton Sun* library and April Bartlett of the *St. Albert Gazette* for allowing me to use photographs for which they hold copyright. In addition, I wish to thank individuals who gave me personal photographs to use in order to enhance the written text of this book: Dr. Lorne Tyrrell, Gerald Robertson, Frank Kozar, the Davies Family, the Grant Mitchell family and Rod Stewart, a member of the Royal Canadian Legion. I thank Bernie Roessler of Plumbheavy Design who was most patient with me and created the splendid design on both front and back covers of this book. I also thank the talented Darren Shaw who was essential in placing the pictures within the text and creating the inside design of the book. Finally, I am very appreciative of the encouragement of the Honourable Lois Hole, former Lieutenant-Governor of Alberta, who never lost faith that this project would come to a successful conclusion.

I offer this book to the people of Alberta as my personal centennial project.

Kenneth Munro
Edmonton, Alberta
November 2004

# PREFACE

# THE MAPLE CROWN IN ALBERTA

The opening of each Session of the Legislature of Alberta represents the supreme moment of our province's political life. This splendid ritual takes place regularly in the capital when the Crown's representative in the province reads *The Speech from the Throne.* The Lieutenant-Governor arrives at the Legislature grounds, and as he alights from a carriage or car a 15-gun salute booms out over the river valley. Then he inspects the guard of honour, outside if the weather permits, inside the rotunda of the Legislature Building if the weather is too cold. Greeted by the gentlemen escort, the Lieutenant-Governor proceeds to the Vice-regal offices on the third floor of the Legislature to prepare for the entry into the Legislative Chamber itself.

When the Lieutenant-Governor enters the Assembly Chamber, a trumpet fanfare sounds from the galleries to signal the beginning of this ceremony rooted in history, pomp and pageantry. Walking to the dias situated against the south wall of the Legislative Chamber, the Lieutenant-Governor takes his place on the throne and presides over the Crown's court in Alberta. The Premier is on the right flanked by members of the government in their places. The leader of Her Majesty's Loyal Opposition and other opposition members are on the left. Facing the Lieutenant-Governor is the Chief Justice of the Alberta Court of Appeal and filling the Legislative Assembly Chamber are people in formal dress and varied uniforms, including members of the consular

iv

(Public Archives of Alberta, PA.5233/1)

> The Speech from the Throne
> His Honour Grant MacEwan reads The Speech from the Throne at the Opening of the Alberta Legislature, 13 February 1969

corps, bishops, and the President of the University of Alberta. Gathered around the throne and wearing their aquillettes and medals, are the Gentlemen Escorts who historically have accompanied the Sovereign to Parliament as protection.

The Escort includes senior Officers of the Armed Forces, the Assistant Commissioner of K-Division of the Royal Canadian Mounted Police, the Chief of the Edmonton Police Service, the Lieutenant-Governor's Aides-de-Camp and Private Secretary. A little below, on His Honour's right, stands the Speaker of the Legislative Assembly in black robes and tricorn hat and the Sergeant at Arms of the Legislature who carries the Black Rod into the Assembly at the head of the Vice-regal procession. All those with power and authority over us are gathered together before the throne to hear a message from the Queen's representative in Alberta. This ceremony reminds us that we live in a constitutional monarchy whereby the Sovereign personifies the state.

# I
# THE MAPLE CROWN

Constitutional Monarchy

Canada is the only monarchy, other than Belize, in all of continental America. The Canadian Crown is a constitutional monarchy made manifest in a team of persons: the Monarch who lives outside the country and who joins us in a world-wide community with peoples of different place, ethnicity, and creed, the Governor General who resides in Ottawa and exercises all prerogatives of the Crown within the federal sphere of jurisdiction, and the ten Lieutenant-Governors who reside in their respective provincial capitals and exercise the prerogatives of the Crown within the provincial sphere of jurisdiction.[1] For Canada, the majesty of the Monarch inspires the office of the Governor General who expresses the ideals of the country as a whole, and the office of the ten Lieutenant-Governors who combine their respective provincial character with the essential qualities necessary to make this institution relevant. The Crown represents "to the people a symbol of themselves, not necessarily as they are but as they would want themselves to be."[2]

Canadians are a parliamentary people; sovereignty lies with the Queen in Parliament. Canada has not been born through revolution, but rather through parliamentary debate and discussion. Consequently, all significant occurrences in our political life take place in Parliament and are sanctioned by the Crown. In October 1964, Queen Elizabeth II said that the role of the constitutional monarch "is to personify the democratic state, to sanction legitimate authority, to assure the legality of its measures, and to guarantee the execution of the popular will. In accomplishing this task, it protects the people against disorder."[3]

*The Hereditary Monarch*, Her Majesty Queen Elizabeth II, Queen of Canada, embodies Canada and is the Canadian Head of State. To Canadians, Queen Elizabeth is an international symbol and her "appeal is to values that burst beyond the limits of nationality." [4] In 1953, Elizabeth II was proclaimed at Ottawa on 29 May: " Elizabeth the Second, by the Grace of God of the United Kingdom, Canada and her other Realms and Territories Queen, Head of the Commonwealth, Defender of the Faith."[5] She represents our highest ideals, all that is best and most cherished by Canadians. Since not everyone can sit on the throne, she does that for us. Thus, when Canadians cheer the Queen, they are really cheering each other; when Canadians sing the "Royal Anthem" *God Save the Queen,* they are really saying "God help us to govern ourselves."[6] The Queen embodies the hope that at the centre of the modern technocratic and impersonal state there is a human being.

As Head of State, the Queen is "the living symbol of the roots and continuity of our country and of our institutions."[7] Queen Elizabeth II reminds us of

> the principles according to which we Canadians understand our Government should be conducted, how the powers of the state should be arranged for our safety and protection. Without the Queen of Canada, without the sacredness and otherness of royalty, without her articulating the importance of the spiritual dimension in people's lives, the office of the Governor-General (to whom in fact her constitutional powers and prerogatives have

been transferred) and that of the Lieutenant-Governors would be seriously weakened. She is the one entrusted with the conscience of the nation.[8]

The Queen maintains several important functions as Head of State of Canada. Most importantly, she appoints the Governor General on the advice of the Canadian Prime Minister.[9] In addition, under the *Constitution Act, 1867*, the Queen decides the seat of government of Canada, (Section 16) and on the advice of the Governor General, may add four to eight members to the Senate of Canada (Section 26). This procedure was followed in the fall of 1990 when Prime Minister Brian Mulroney did not have a majority to pass his Goods and Services Tax (GST) legislation through the Liberal dominated Senate. Like her father, King George VI, who personally assented to Bills in the Canadian Senate in 1939, she performs other constitutional functions when in Canada. She personally opened the Canadian Parliament in 1957 and 1977 and proclaimed the Constitution Act, 1982 on 17 April 1982 in Ottawa. She has been present at formal meetings of her Canadian Privy Council. As Canadian Head of State, she opened the Olympic Games in Montreal (1976) and the Commonwealth Games in Edmonton (1978) and the Commonwealth Games in Victoria, British Columbia (1994).

From time to time, the Canadian government asks the Queen to carry out other functions on behalf of the Canadian people. At the request of Prime Minister John Diefenbaker, Her Majesty visited the United States as Queen of Canada in 1957 following a visit to Ottawa. Her Majesty was proud to take on a fence mending mission and to bask in the success her country had

## Proclamation of Constitution Act, 1982
Her Majesty Queen Elizabeth II proclaims the Constitution Act, 1982, on Parliament Hill 17 April 1982

(Robert Cooper, National Archives of Canada, PA141503)

## Commonwealth Games 1978
Her Majesty Queen Elizabeth II and HRH The Duke of Edinburgh arrive at Commonwealth Stadium at Edmonton for the opening of the Commonwealth Games, 3 August 1978

(Courtesy of Davies Family)

*Commonwealth Games, Edmonton 1978*
Queen Elizabeth II, accompanied by Prince Philip and Prince Edward, are escorted to the shooting venue by host Edward (Red) Davies

achieved by healing the breech in relations which had developed between the United States on the one hand, and France and Britain on the other during the Suez Crisis of 1956. One of her former Minister's of External Affairs, Lester B. Pearson, had just the day previously been awarded the Nobel Peace Prize for suggesting the use of peace keeping troops along the length of the Suez canal. Not only did this solution to a prickly diplomatic problem raise the profile of the United Nations, but it began a new and much-respected role for Her Majesty's

Canadian Armed Forces.

Then in 1970, while her Prime Minister, Pierre Elliott Trudeau exercised power, the Queen agreed to visit the Arctic following a dispute with the Americans over whether the North West Passage was within Canadian territorial waters. Her Majesty set out to make the world understand that this disputed passage lay within Canada's jurisdiction and that if the Americans wished to send super oil tankers such as *the Manhattan* through the North West Passage from Prudhoe Bay in Alaska to the lower 48 states as they did in 1969,[10] permission from Canada would first have to be obtained. The international press which follows the royal family ensured that Canada's message received world-wide attention with the Queen's arrival at Frobisher Bay (today called Iqaluit) in early July.[11] Pictures of the Queen showing the Canadian flag by hopping across the North in the crisp Arctic air from Frobisher Bay to Inuvik via Resolute Bay, were visible proof that "This Land is Our Land"![12] In reaction to the Americans' insistence that the Northwest Passage was International Water, by 1977, Canada had declared a 200-mile fishing and resource zone extending from our shores. The Queen's visit to the Arctic seven years earlier was essential to indicate to the world that this land and the water between the Arctic islands belonged to Canada. On these occasions, the Queen was working on behalf of her Canadian people.

In addition, the Monarch often represents Canadians at war cemeteries and monuments to our war dead overseas. For example, in 1936, King Edward VIII went to Vimy Ridge in France to inaugurate the memorial to the Canadian dead of the First World War.[13] This site of one of the bloodiest

(National Archives of Canada, PA148881)

### Unveiling of Vimy Ridge Monument
His Majesty King Edward VIII attends ceremonies unveiling the monument at Vimy Ridge, July 1936

battles of that war had been designated Canadian territory by the French government. On 3 June 1994, the Queen attended the ceremony at London's Green Park, a royal park, where she unveiled a memorial honouring Canada's role in the two world wars in the presence of ten members of the Royal Family and her Canadian Prime Minister, The Right Honourable Jean Chrétien.[14] Again, as Queen of Canada, Her Majesty Queen Elizabeth presided over the ceremony at Juno Beach in Normandy, France on 6 June 2004, to commemorate the 60$^{th}$ anniversary of D-Day. As our Queen, she spoke to Canadian veterans and laid a wreath at the Canadian memorial at Juno Beach.[15]

In addition to the Monarch, the Governor General embodies a second

(Tom Hanson, Canadian Press)

### 60th Anniversary of D-Day
Queen Elizabeth II listens with Prime Minister Paul Martin as Governor General Adrian Clarkson speaks at a ceremony marking the 60th anniversary of D-Day in Courseulles-sur-Mer, France, 6 June 2004

aspect of Canada's Maple Crown. Although the Queen is Canadian head of state, "almost all of the constitutional tasks of head of state can be done by the governor-general only."[16]

*The Governor General* represents the Queen for all Canadians and is really "the principal symbol of unity and continuity in the country."[17] While Canadians have always lived under a monarchical system of government since the time of contact with the First Nations, the Office of Governor General is the only uninterrupted, continuous institution we have which dates back to those early beginnings. The Office of Governor General was most fully defined through the granting of the Letters Patent by King George VI and proclaimed on 1 October 1947. These Letters marked the final constitutional step in the transfer of royal powers from the Monarch to the Governor General. They authorized the Governor General "to exercise all power and authority" lawfully belonging to the Crown in Canada.[18] Following the Queen's visit to Canada in 1977, Her Majesty agreed to allow the Governor General to exercise the royal prerogative in all areas of Canada's international relations such as the declaration of war, the signing of letters of credence for Canada's ambassadors and high commissioners, and the ratification of treaties.[19]

The Letters Patent of 1947, in effect, also transferred to Governors General the duty to represent Canada abroad. The first such occasion occurred in 1926 when Lord Willingdon visited Washington.[20] In 1969, Governor General Roland Michener made the first state visit to the Caribbean as a representative of the Canadian Head of State[21] and since that time, the Governor General, rather than the Queen, has often represented Canada abroad. In a speech delivered in Toronto, the Right Honourable Adrienne Clarkson quoted the Queen who has encouraged her Governors General to go abroad and visit as Canadian Head of State.[22] Following the Queen's advice, the Canadian government encouraged His Excellency the Right Honourable Edward Schreyer to make a Canadian state visit to the Scandinavian countries, and Finland and Iceland, during late May and early June 1981[23] and the Right Honourable Adrienne Clarkson did the same, visiting Germany and Argentina in 2001. To promote things Canadian abroad, in October 2003, Governor General Adrienne Clarkson undertook a Polar nations trip on behalf of Canada, visiting Russia, Finland, and Iceland under the auspices of the Department of Foreign Affairs.[24] On a more local level, the Lieutenant-Governors express the third aspect of the Canadian Crown.

*The Lieutenant-Governors* participate fully in the provincial aspects of the Crown's sovereignty. In the beginning, there was much ambiguity about the office of Lieutenant-Governor. The Fathers of Confederation first agreed that the Lieutenant Governor was to be a "federal officer", that is, a representative of the federal government who would act as an intermediary between Ottawa and the provincial administrations. Consequently, Lieutenant-Governors were to be appointed by the Governor General and not the Monarch.[25] The federal government would pay the Lieutenant-Governor's salary and the Governor General, on the advice of the Canadian Prime Minister, could dismiss him.[26] On behalf of the federal government, Lieutenant-Governors would have authority to veto or reserve bills which they might not consider to be in the interests of the whole country.[27]   This subordination of the office is revealed in the manner the Lieutenant-Governor is addressed:  since the time of Lord Dufferin, Lieutenant-Governors have been addressed as "Your Honour" rather than "Your Excellency" as is Governor General.   On the other hand, the Fathers of Confederation granted the Lieutenant-Governors a great seal, which is the main instrument and symbol of sovereign authority, and it authorized them to act in the Queen's name.[28]

Shortly after Confederation, Sir Oliver Mowat when Premier of Ontario, attempted to remove this notion of subordination and initiated a series of court cases which eventually brought the Judicial Committee of the Privy Council in 1892 to recognize the Lieutenant-Governors as full representatives of the Crown for all purposes of provincial jurisdiction.[29] In the case of *Liquidators of the Maritime Bank v. Receiver General of New Brunswick* (1892), the court ruled that "'the Lieutenant-Governor...[was] as much a representative of His Majesty for all purposes of Provincial Government as is the Governor-General for all purposes of Dominion Government.'"[30]  Thus, by the late nineteenth century, the Crown was made the legal and constitutional link between the different parts of Canada.  Subsequent judicial decision, custom, convention and evolution have strengthened this bond.  Since the Queen reigns in right of each province as well as of Canada as a whole, the phrase "Her Majesty (or the Crown) in right of Alberta" frequently occurs in the constitutional and legal documents of the province.

The Lieutenant-Governor therefore, acts with respect to the province just as the Governor General does for Canada, and exercises all of the Queen's powers within provincial jurisdiction. The Lieutenant-Governor, and the provincial Crown which the Lieutenant-Governor personifies, symbolizes the sovereignty of the provincial government within Confederation. The direct link with the Sovereign is essential to the constitutional status of the provinces in the federal state; for the provinces derive sovereignty over their own constitutionally-allocated powers, not from the federal Parliament or the Governor General, but from the Crown and the Queen.[31] As her term of office was coming to an end, the former Lieutenant-Governor of Ontario, the Honourable Hilary M. Weston, defined this new reality. In a speech before the Canadian Club of Toronto, she noted that "Though we are appointed by Ottawa, we are no longer its agent nor some sort of local assistant to the Governor-General. Rather, we are the legal personifications of jurisdictions, such as education and health, in which the provinces are autonomous and sovereign."[32] Under the terms of the *Constitution Act, 1867,* the Lieutenant-Governor is appointed for a minimum period of five years, which may be extended, and remains in office until a successor is appointed and installed.[33]

In effect, in Canada, the sovereignty of the Crown is exercised by different representatives in different jurisdictions; diversity is reconciled to unity. Canada thus maintains a fundamental and historic distinction between the Crown and government—between the Queen who is the embodiment of Canada and the *Head of State,* and the *Head of Government* (the Prime Minister or Premier). Although the repository of all power, the Crown is almost completely powerless. The Monarch reigns but does not rule. It is the Prime Minister and Premiers who wield this power as long as they have the majority votes in the elected body of the Federal Parliament, or the Assembly in the provinces. The Crown ensures that these individuals know their place as trustees of power which does not belong to them. "The people and their Parliament can control the head of government because he cannot identify himself with the state or confuse loyalty to himself with allegiance to the state."[34]

To make any changes respecting "the office of the Queen, the Governor General and the Lieutenant Governor of a province" authorization can only occur by resolutions of the Senate and House of Commons and of the Legislative Assembly of each province. (Section 41, *Constitution Act, 1982*) This constitutional necessity means that Canada will remain a constitutional monarchy well into the foreseeable future and the Queen will remain at the top of the tables of precedence for Canada and the provinces.

For Canada, the Queen is immediately followed by the Governor General; however, the Lieutenant-Governors are placed below the Prime Minister and the various Ministers of the federal government. In 1867, the Lieutenant-Governors ranked immediately behind the Governor General and the senior officer commanding British military forces. Over time, however, Lieutenant-Governors have fallen in the table of precedence for Canada. Since the Royal Visit of King George VI and Queen Elizabeth in 1939, on all occasions the Canadian Prime Minister takes precedence over Lieutenant-Governors and at federal functions, so do federal cabinet ministers.[35]

*Table of precedence for Canada*

The Queen
Governor General
Canadian Prime Minister
Canadian cabinet ministers
Lieutenant-Governors

In the provinces, the Lieutenant-Governors follow the Queen in order of precedence.

*Alberta Table of Precedence*

The Queen
The Lieutenant Governor
The Premier
The Chief Justice of Alberta
Former Lieutenant-Governors
Former Premiers
The Speaker of the Legislative Assembly[36]

When the Lieutenant-Governor is out of the province or is unable to carry out essential functions of the office, the *Administrator* of the province performs the Lieutenant-Governor's necessary constitutional tasks. The Governor General through an Order-in-Council appoints an Administrator "to execute the Office and Functions of Lieutenant Governor during his Absence, Illness, or other Inability."[37] In Alberta, the Chief Justice of the Alberta Court of Appeals is generally the Administrator of the province. The Administrator serves only during the term of a specific Lieutenant-Governor and must be re-appointed or another individual found to carry out the Administrator's responsibilities when a new Lieutenant-Governor assumes office.

The position of Administrator is extremely important. When His Honour Philip Primrose became ill shortly after assuming office, the Administrator, Chief Justice Horace Harvey had to assume his functions such as signing Orders-in-Council and on 25 February 1937, read the Speech from the Throne to open a new Legislative session.[38]

(Provincial Archives of Alberta, Ks.5/2)

### The Administrator
Chief Justice Harvey, acting as Administrator in the absence of Lieutenant-Governor Primrose, reads the Speech from the Throne, 25 February 1937

A constitutional question arose concerning the office of Administrator in March 1937 because of the death of His Honour Philip Primrose while in office and the Legislature was sitting. Political pundits were baffled and many thought that for the first time in Canadian history a Lieutenant-Governor had died in office while the Legislative Assembly was still in session. Although Justice Harvey had been appointed Administrator during the illness of Lieutenant-Governor Primrose, his appointment had lapsed with His Honour's death on Wednesday 17 March. As a result, no Orders-in-Council could be passed and no money bills could be introduced into the Legislative Assembly because no prior consent could be given by the Lieutenant-Governor or Administrator. In addition, the fiscal year was about to end on 31 March and from that day forward the government was unable to spend in the next fiscal year. When Premier Aberhart informed Ottawa about this awkward situation, he discovered that the Prime Minister, Mackenzie King was absent from the capital for five days and thus could not advise the Governor General on the appointment of a new Lieutenant-Governor until his return.[39] Albertans were unaware that a similar situation had occurred in Quebec in 1929.

As Sir Lomer Gouin, the Lieutenant-Governor of Quebec prepared to leave his Legislature office to go to prorogue the Legislative Session in the Upper House, he dropped dead of a heart attack. Consequently, the Assembly members had to return to the Lower House where the Speaker duly adjourned the session. Sir Lomer Gouin's state funeral took place and a new Vice-regal representative was named. Immediately following his installation as the new Lieutenant-Governor of the province of Quebec on 4 April 1929, the Honourable Henry G. Carroll prorogued the Legislature.[40] Alberta would put right the break in the machinery of government in a similar fashion.

Following the death of the Honourable Philip Primrose, the Alberta Legislature adjourned until the following Tuesday and a state funeral was held for His Honour. As soon as the Canadian Prime Minister returned to Ottawa and met with the Governor General, the Governor General announced that John Bowen would become Alberta's next Lieutenant-Governor. Minutes before the Legislative Assembly resumed its sitting, His Honour John Bowen was installed as the King's Vice-regal representative in the Lieutenant-Governor's office in the Legislature Building.[41] Government could continue to function once again and a new Administrator could now be appointed.

The Administrator came to public view again in 1948. Because His Honour John Bowen was too ill to perform his official duties, the Administrator, Chief Justice Horace Harvey of the Appellate Division, read the Speech from the Throne at the opening of the Legislature on 19 February.[42] More recently, in February 1996 when His Honour Gordon Towers was confined to bed with pneumonia and could not open the Legislative Session by reading of the Speech from the Throne, the Administrator, Justice John "Buzz" McClung performed that constitutional role for him.[43]

In an earlier period, the Honourable George B. O'Connor, Chief Justice of the Supreme Court of Alberta, assumed the role of Administrator when His Honour John Bowlen left to attend the coronation of Queen Elizabeth II.[44] When His Honour Percy Page travelled to Florida for his vacation each spring, Chief Justice S. Bruce Smith, as Administrator, assumed the constitutional role normally performed by the Lieutenant-Governor.[45] At the beginning of the twenty-first century, Madame Justice Catherine Fraser normally takes on those

(City of Edmonton Archives, EA600-816c)

(City of Edmonton Archives, EA600-816a)

### The Administrator
Chief Justice Harvey, acting as Administrator in the absence of
Lieutenant-Governor Bowen, reads the Speech from the Throne
19 February 1948

(Walter Tychnowicz, *Edmonton Sun*)

## The Administrator
The Honourable Mr. Justice John "Buzz" McClung read the Speech from the Throne 13 February 1996 as Administrator of the Province of Alberta because of the illness of Lieutenant-Governor Gordon Towers

responsibilities each time Her Honour Lois Hole leaves the province.

The Monarch and Lieutenant-Governors
*Visit to the Sovereign*

Although Lieutenant-Governors have continued to be appointees of the Governor General and to hold some residual federal powers, over time they have come to be seen as the Sovereign's direct and personal representatives in their respective provinces. By acting in the name of the Queen in right of the province, it was only natural that Lieutenant-Governors should have a direct link with the Sovereign by visiting the Monarch during their term of office. This visit was a consequence of the phenomenon of province-building and consequently, an indication that the provincial Crown's powers and status have grown as provincial power has increased since Confederation.[46]

In 1956, His Honour John Bowlen was in London and invited to Buckingham Palace for a private audience with the Queen. This visit resulted from the Queen's preparedness "to receive each Lieutenant-governor and his wife once during his term of office" and Her Majesty requested "that this audience should take place as soon as possible after his appointment...."[47] The audience between His Honour and Her Majesty occurred on Thursday, 28 June 1956[48] and was the first time a Lieutenant-Governor from a Dominion ever received such an invitation.[49] This visit set an important precedence. It also indicated the increasing importance of the Office of Lieutenant-Governor within the context of the Canadian Crown. Since that time, a visit to the Monarch by a Lieutenant-Governor has become a matter of custom upon assuming office.

The visit of His Honour Ralph Steinhauer to the Queen in 1976 at first appeared to take on a political complexion. He decided to have Alberta Indian chiefs, the Canadian High Commissioner and Alberta's Attorney General accompany him for the occasion. The Governor General's private secretary, Esmond Butler, informed the Lieutenant-Governor that the federal government wanted assurances the visit would not be used "'to draw attention to problems which are of concern to the Indian people of this country.'" Only on that condition being met would the Governor General on the advice of the Prime Minister, approve the visit of the Alberta Indian Chiefs to the Queen.[50]

The six chiefs and their wives who accompanied His Honour and his wife to London were there to commemorate the centennial of the signing of Treaties Six (1876) and Seven (1877) between Queen Victoria and the Cree, Blackfoot, Blood, Peigan, Sarcee and Stoney nations.[51] The British press, such as the *Daily Mirror*, could not resist the temptation of glib word plays and announced to British readers under the headline "'pow-wow at the palace'" that "'The Queen was surrounded by red Indians yesterday after they invaded Buckingham Palace. But the Indians - six Canadian chiefs and their squaws weren't on the warpath.'"[52] Although the Chiefs faced ignorance on the part of the British press, such insensitivity was not present at the audience with the Queen.

His Honour Frank Lynch-Staunton decided to pay his visit to the Queen in 1983. Since the Honourable Irwin MacIntosh was finishing up his term of office in Saskatchewan, but had never visited the Queen, the two decided to go together. His Honour was invited to Windsor Castle for lunch on 13 April.[53] Protocol was observed: since Saskatchewan was one week older than Alberta, the Lieutenant-Governor from Saskatchewan sat on the Queen's right while His Honour Frank Lynch-Staunton sat on her left. Lunching with the Queen was a distinctive privilege since previous Lieutenant-Governors were only accorded a one-half hour audience with Her Majesty.[54]

Although not reported in the press back home, Her Honour Helen Hunley remembered her visit with the Queen in 1988 as the highlight of her term of office.[55] Although the Honourable "Bud" Olson did not visit the Queen because of poor health, Her Honour Lois Hole flew to Britain in the fall of 2000 with much publicity.[56] On the airplane from Calgary to London she

(Associated Press Photo, Fiona Hanson, WPA Pool)

**Visit to The Queen**
The Queen welcomes Her Honour Lois Hole to Buckingham Palace
1 November 2000

met an Albertan who was going to Norway to work in the computer business. When he asked her where she was going, she replied: "I'm going to London to visit the Queen." As memories of the famous nursery rhyme[57] flashed into his mind, he broke out in gales of laughter, not believing a word she said. How wrong he proved to be!

*The Crown Made Visible*

Because the Lieutenant-Governor also visits the Queen on the occasion of her special trips to Canada's capital, even if Her Majesty does not come to Alberta or her other provinces, such occasions allow the Canadian Crown to become visible as all its constituent parts assemble physically in one place. On 14 October 1957 when Her Majesty The Queen became the first Canadian reigning Monarch to Open Parliament and again on 18 October 1977 during Her Majesty's Silver Jubilee visit to Canada, the Sovereign, Governor General and Lieutenant-Governors were all present for these special occasions. In 1957, His Honour John Bowlen not only attended the historic Opening of Parliament, but also went to the state dinner at Rideau Hall.[58] In 1977, Lieutenant-Governors joined the Governor General at a state dinner hosted by Her Majesty The Queen to celebrate her Silver Jubilee.[59] Again, during the centennial year of Confederation, all of the Lieutenant-Governors and the Governor General travelled to Kingston where The Queen and Prince Philip gave a state dinner aboard the royal yacht Britannia on 4 July 1967. His Honour Grant MacEwan and his wife were present for that function.[60] When the Queen came to Canada 17 April 1982 to proclaim the *Constitution Act,*

*1982* on Parliament Hill, Alberta's Lieutenant-Governor, the Honourable Frank Lynch-Staunton, joined Her Majesty and his other Vice-regal colleagues for this historic and splendid occasion.[61]

*Correspondence*

Although Lieutenant-Governors have the opportunity to visit the Queen at least once during their term of office, Lieutenant-Governors never correspond directly with the Monarch except on personal matters such as sending Christmas greetings. All correspondence is routed via the Secretary of State or the Governor General. In the early years of Confederation, there was no need for a direct relationship between these two aspects of the Crown. Over the years, this situation has changed as Lieutenant-Governors have developed a closer tie to the Sovereign through the right of one visit during a term of office and visits by the Monarch to individual provinces. Nevertheless, correspondence is still largely confined to personal greetings and expressions of thanks rather than formal administrative correspondence. For example, during her audience with the Queen in November 2000, Her Honour Lois Hole presented Her Majesty with a gardening book and also asked her to pass one on to Prince Charles. Her Honour Lois Hole received a hand-written letter from the Prince of Wales thanking her for her thoughtfulness. When she opened the letter she was deeply moved and has kept it in her personal safe at home for posterity. At Christmas that same year, Her Majesty Queen Elizabeth sent a personally signed Christmas card to Her Honour and the Prince of Wales also sent Christmas greetings.

Governor General and Lieutenant-Governors

The relationship between Lieutenant-Governors and the Governor General is much closer than the relationship between the Monarch and Lieutenant-Governors. Besides receiving their appointments from the Governor General, on the advice of the Canadian Prime Minister, Lieutenant-Governors must ask permission from the Governor General to leave the province for any reason during their term of office. When a Governor General is appointed, an official visit is made to each provincial capital at which time the Lieutenant-Governor greets their Excellencies on behalf of all citizens of the province.

*Greeting the Governor General*

(City of Edmonton Archives, EA10-786)

His Honour George Bulyea greets the Duke of Connaught, 1911

(Glenbow Archives, NC-6-2948)

His Honour Robert Brett greets the Duke of Devonshire, 1917

(Glenbow Archives, ND-3-6968d)

His Honour William Walsh greets Governor General Lord Bessborough, 1935

(City of Edmonton Archives, EA-600-234H)

His Honour John Bowen welcomes Governor General Viscount Alexander of Tunis and Lady Alexander to Edmonton, 1947

With little secretarial or other personnel in support of the office, the Lieutenant-Governor of Alberta has limited expertise from whom to seek advice. The Governor General's court is much more extensive and offers guidance. Such assistance became more institutionalized during the term of office of His Excellency Roland Michener. He decided to bring his provincial Vice-regal colleagues together to discuss matters which would help all royal representatives in Canada. He observed that while the Prime Minster and provincial Premiers had regular federal-provincial meetings, the Governor General and Lieutenant-Governors never met. Consequently, he began regular consultations with the Lieutenant-Governors of Canada.

The first of these meetings took place in 1973. The Right Honourable Roland Michener invited all Lieutenant-Governors to a November conference at Rideau Hall. All Vice-regal representatives in Canada went to Ottawa except Grant MacEwan from Alberta who had a prior commitment. At this meeting, they discussed their constitutional responsibilities as well as the way to discharge their unofficial and ceremonial functions. Michener saw that there were papers and documents prepared for the meeting and that constitutional authorities came to talk to the group.[62] Instituted at the very end of Michener's term, these consultations began as a biennial affair but later developed into an annual occurrence.[63]

Through discussions at these conferences, the new Lieutenant-Governor's flags were suggested and adopted by most provincial Lieutenant-Governors. During The Honourable "Bud" Olson's term of office, the idea of moving the New Years Levee was broached and adopted by the Governor General and a few of the Lieutenant-Governors, including His Honour. Before attending her first meeting, Lois Hole said that she would be lobbying the Governor General and other Lieutenant-Governors to speak out on the issue of education, particularly liberal arts education, because she feels so strongly about this issue. The 2001 conference concluded at Quebec City in September just as the "terrorist crisis" erupted with the destruction of the World Trade Centre towers in New York city. With all air traffic stopped in North America, Her Honour made her way back to Alberta on a special provincially chartered flight which was shared with Manitoba's Lieutenant-Governor and Alberta and Saskatchewan cabinet ministers once federal aviation authorities had given the green light for planes on government business to take off.[64]

*Aides-de-Camp*

Whenever the Lieutenant-Governor travels about the province on official business, she is accompanied on all of these occasions by an aide-de-camp who acts as an assistant. These positions are Honourary and the individuals assuming these responsibilities are appointed by the Lieutenant-Governor from the Regular Forces, Reservists and the Royal Canadian Mounted Police. The Aides-de-Camp normally continue in their position during the term of office of

(Photo Courtesy of Lt Col Frank Kozar, Edmonton)

### Aide-de-Camp
Her Honour's Aide-de-Camp escorts Lieutenant-Governor Lois Hole into the Queen's Jubilee Banquet, 6 February 2002

the Lieutenant-Governor who appoints them. All of these personnel were male until 1975 when an Edmonton militia and nursing officer, Captain Donna Lynch, became the first woman to serve as aide-de-camp to an Alberta Lieutenant-Governor.[65]

The Aides-de-Camp wear gold braid on the right shoulder of their uniform, the aiguillette. They are entitled to wear the aiguillette whenever they attend the same function as the Lieutenant-Governor even though they may not be on duty for that function.

Expenditure on Office of Lieutenant-Governor

To carry out their official duties, Lieutenant-Governors must spend public monies. According to the Public Accounts for the 2000-2001 fiscal year, Alberta spends approximately $199,000 on the Office of Lieutenant-Governor. This figure is somewhat deceiving since Alberta does not apply every charge to the Lieutenant-Governor's budget. The Lieutenant-Governor shares many facilities with other departments of government, primarily the Executive Council. Therefore, the Alberta government budgets only for items such as Office salaries, equipment and supplies, for the lease of the official car and its fuel.[66] For example, the Alberta government, until 2004, paid for an official residence with one residence staff member, and continues to pay for an office in the Legislature with two office staff and an official car.[67] The current Alberta Lieutenant-Governor, Her Honour Lois Hole, never occupied the former residence, but chose to remain in her own home at St. Albert during her term of office. The federal government pays the salary of the Lieutenant-Governor and the federal share of expenses of the Office. The Department of Canadian Heritage also provides pensions for former Lieutenant-Governors.[68]

# NOTES

1. Jacques Monet, s.j. "The Queen Opens Parliament", in *The Silver Jubilee: Royal Visit to Canada,* Ottawa: Deneau & Greenberg, 1977, 38.

2. *St. John's Edmonton Report,* 8 July 1974, 10.

3. Frank MacKinnon, *The Crown in Canada,* [Calgary]: Glenbow-Alberta Institute, McClelland and Stewart West, [1976], 27.

4. Jacques Monet, s.j. "The Queen Opens Parliament", 38.

5. Robert MacGregor Dawson, *The Government of Canada,* third edition revised, Toronto: University of Toronto Press, [1957], 63.

6. MacKinnon, *The Crown in Canada,* 13.

7. Jacques Monet, sj "Canada's Elizabethan Jubilee: Reflections on the Queen of Canada", *Canadian Monarchist News,* 7.2 (Autumn 2002), 11; and reprinted in *National Post,* Saturday 12 October 2002, B3.

8. *Ibid.*, B3.

9. Eugene Forsey, "The Role and Position of the Monarch in Canada", *The Parliamentarian,* 64.1 (January 1983), 11.

10. Richard Gwyn, *The Northern Magus,* [Toronto]: McClelland & Stewart, [1980], 301.

11. Charles Lynch, *Edmonton Journal,* 6 July 1970, A2.

12. *Edmonton Journal,* 7 July 1970, A1.

13. Philip Zeigler, *King Edward VIII,* London: Collins, 1990, 266.

14. *Maclean's* 6 June 1994, Vol. 107, No. 23, 23; *Edmonton Journal,* 4 June 1994, A3.

15. Michael Valpy, "A Queen and her agent may mix", *Globe and Mail,* Tuesday, 8 June 2004.

16. *Ibid.*

17. Jacques Monet, s.j. "The Queen Opens Parliament", 38.

18. Eugene Forsey, "The Role and Position of the Monarch in Canada", *The Parliamentarian, Journal of the Parliaments of the Commonwealth,* 64.1 (January 1983), 11.

19. David E. Smith, *The Invisible Crown: The First Principle of Canadian Government,* Toronto: University of Toronto Press, [1995], 46; Eugene Forsey, "The Role and Position of the Monarch in Canada", *The Parliamentarian,* 64.1 (January 1983), 11; Jules Léger, Governor General of Canada 1974-1979, [Montreal]: La Presse, [1982], 214.

20. Her Excellency the Right Honourable Adrienne Clarkson, "Address at the University of Toronto Faculty Association's C. B. Macpherson Lecture", Wednesday, 31 March 2004.

21. Forsey, "The Role and Position of the Monarch in Canada", *The Parliamentarian,* 64.1 (January 1983),47.

22. Her Excellency the Right Honourable Adrienne Clarkson, "Address at the University of Toronto Faculty Association's C. B. Macpherson Lecture", Wednesday, 31 March 2004.

23. Claire Mowat, *Pomp and Circumstances,* Toronto: Seal edition, McClelland-Bantam, [1992], 37 & 319.

24. *National Post,* Tuesday, 6 April 2004, A15; John Aimers, "Clarkson is getting a bum rap" in *National Post,* Tuesday, 16 March 2004, A15.

25. *The British North America Act, 1867* in J.L. Finlay and D.N. Sprague, *The Structure of Canadian History,* 5th edition, Scarborough, Ontario: Prentice Hall Allyn and Bacon Canada, [1997], Section 58, 618.

26. *Ibid.,* Sections 59 and 60, 618.

27. *Ibid.,* Section 55, 617 and Section 90, 624.

28. Conrad Swan, *Canada: Symbols of Sovereignty,* Toronto: University of Toronto Press, [1977], 33&212.

29. John T. Saywell, *The Office of Lieutenant-Governor: A Study in Canadian Government and Politics,* Toronto: University of Toronto Press, 1957, 14. Also see, A. Margaret Evans, *Sir Oliver Mowat,* Toronto: University of Toronto Press, [1992], 148, 154,176,178-9.

30. *Liquidators of the Maritime Bank v. Receiver General of New Brunswick* (1892) AC 437 as cited in Smith, *The Invisible Crown,* 9.

31. MacKinnon, *The Crown in Canada*, 91.

32. *The National Post,* 10 December 2001, A4.

33. *The Constitution Act, 1867,* in Finlay and Sprague, Section 59, 618.

34. MacKinnon, *The Crown in Canada*,

35. Saywell, *Office of Lieutenant-Governor,* 17-18.

36. "Table of Precedence for Alberta" www.canadianheritage.gc.ca/progs/cpsc-ccsp/atc-ac/precab_e.cfm

37. *The British North America Act, 1867,* section 67 as cited in Finlay and Sprague, 620.

38. *Edmonton Journal,* Wednesday 24 February 1937, 1 and Thursday 25 February 1937, 17.

39. *Edmonton Journal,* Wednesday 17 March 1937,1.

40. *Montreal Gazette,* Friday 29 March 1929, 1; Friday 5 April 1929, 1; Robert Rumilly, *Histoire de la province de Québec, Camillien Houde,* Vol. XXX, Montréal: Fides, [1958], 202-206.

41. *Edmonton Journal,* Monday 22 March 1937.

42. *Edmonton Journal,* Thursday 19 February 1948,1 and Friday 20 February, 1.

43. Edmonton *Sun,* Wednesday 14 February 1996, 3.

44. *Edmonton Bulletin,* Tuesday, 12 May 1953.

45. Provincial Archives of Alberta, Correspondence between Lieutenant-Governors, GS 79.338 Box 9, Office of Lieutenant-Governor, letter from Lieutenant-Governor to Chief Justice, the Honourable S. Bruce Smith, 9 April 1965.

46. Smith, *The Invisible Crown,* 54-55.

47. Letter to His Honour John Bowlen from C. Stein, Under Secretary of State, Ottawa, 4 April 1956, *Provincial Archives of Alberta,* Lieutenant-Governors private correspondence 1960-1965, J. Percy Page, GS 84.464 A-1.

48. *The London Times,* Friday, 29 June 1956, 10.

49. A. W. (Tony) Cashman, *The Vice-Regal Cowboy: Life and Times of Alberta's J. J. Bowlen,* Edmonton: The Institute of Applied Art, 1957, 194.

50. Smith, *The Invisible Crown,* 55.

51. *Edmonton Journal,* 30 June 1976, 3.

52. *Ibid.*

53. *The London Times,* Thursday 14 April 1983, 16.

54. Frank Lynch-Staunton, *Greener Pastures: The Memoirs of F. Lynch-Staunton,* Edmonton: Jasper Printing Group, 1987, 42-43.

55. *Edmonton Journal,* 31 December 1990, 1.

56. *Edmonton Journal,* 2 November 2000.

57. The nursery rhyme is as follows:
        Pussy cat, Pussy cat, where have you been?
        I've been to London to look at the Queen.
        Pussy cat, Pussy cat, what did you do there?
        I frightened a little mouse under the chair.
    *Mother Goose Complete Melodies,* Chicago: M.A. Donohue & Co., [1904], 172.

58. *Edmonton Journal,* 18 October 1957.

59. *Edmonton Journal,* Monday 17 October 1977, 3.

60. *Edmonton Journal,* 16 June 1967.

61. *Constitution 1982: Patriation of the Constitution of Canada 1982, a pictorial record,* [Ottawa]: Department of the Secretary of State of Canada, [1983], 108.

62. Peter Stursberg, *Roland Michener: The Last Viceroy,* Toronto: McGraw-Hill Ryerson, [1989], 202-203.

63. *Ibid.,* 203.

64. *Edmonton Journal,* 13 September 2001, A21.

65. *Edmonton Journal,* Monday 21 April 1975, 23.

66. Sean Palmer & John Aimers, "The Cost of Canada's Constitutional Monarchy: $1.10 per Canadian", *Canadian Monarchist News,* 7.2(Autumn 2002), 6.

67. *Ibid.*, 7.

68. *Canadian Monarchist News,* 4.3 (Autumn 1999), 15.

## II
## THE SYMBOLS OF OFFICE

Peoples adopt symbols such as emblems, flags, and systems of awards to express their aspirations and cherished values. Because Canada is a monarchy, the Crown symbolizes our highest ideals as a people. Therefore, it is appropriate that our provincial jurisdictions establish symbols which flow from the Crown. Alberta's royal symbols mirror those of the Crown in other Canadian jurisdictions but reflect the Alberta experience.

Privy Seal of the Lieutenant-Governor

One symbol of Royal authority is the Great Seal of each province which is the emblem of sovereignty, "'the *clavis regni*, the only instrument by which on solemn occasions the will of the sovereign can be expressed. Absolute faith is universally given to every document purporting to be under the Great Seal, as having been duly sealed with it by the authority of the Sovereign.'"[1] With the passage of the Statute of Westminster, the Great Seal of Canada became the supreme token of the sovereign authority for Canada, "that is to say it became the great seal of the monarch in right of Canada—as sovereign of Canada."[2] A new Great Seal is usually brought into being at the beginning of each new reign. Following this practice, the Great Seal of Canada of Her Majesty, Queen Elizabeth II, was brought into being by the Canadian Privy Council and made at the Royal Canadian Mint at Ottawa.[3]

Since Confederation, the tradition within the provinces has been "to have a permanent deputed great seal rather than a new one following the beginning of each new reign."[4] Provincial Great Seals remain "deputed great seals" since they derive their authority from the federal authority of the Crown. However, such provincial seals "are *sui generis* among deputed great seals in that they are tokens of the will of an authority many of whose powers are specified and guaranteed exclusively to them as reserved powers."[5] During the installation ceremonies for Lieutenant-Governors, the Provincial Secretary brings the Great Seal of the Province of Alberta forward and presents it to His Honour committing it to his safe custody. After placing his hand on the Great Seal, the Lieutenant-Governor returns the Great Seal to the Provincial Secretary who acknowledges the trust.[6]

Under British rule and following royal practice in such matters, Governors have used seals which, "while incorporating their own personal arms, are, nevertheless, used in an official capacity. Such are called privy seals."[7] For Acts of the Legislature, Proclamations, Grants and all formal Instruments, the Great Seal of the province must always be used, but for certain other categories such as official appointments made by the Lieutenant-Governor in pursuance of authority vested in him, the Lieutenant-Governor's Privy Seal can be used to authenticate such actions.[8] While the Lieutenant-Governors of some provinces continue to make use of such "Privy Seals", Alberta's Lieutenant-Governors only authenticate official documents and instruments through the use of the Great Seal of the Province. In effect, the Lieutenant-Governor of Alberta possesses a "Privy Seal" but have never used it *ex officio*.[9]

(Provincialk Archives of Alberta, 96-258/85-01247)

*Installation*
Her Honour Helen Hunley was installed as Lieutenant-Governor

22 January 1985

(Public Archives of Alberta, 96-258/85-01236)

## The Great Seal of Alberta
The Great Seal was placed on the desk to the left of the Lieutenant-Governor as she signed the oaths of Office

*Vice-regal Salute*

Besides the Great Seal of a province, the Vice-regal Salute constitutes a symbol of Royal authority. Whenever the Lieutenant-Governor attends an official function where a musical instrument is present or a cassette tape may be played, there is a "Vice-regal Salute" once the official party, that is, the Lieutenant-Governor and her entourage, have arrived. This salute is instrumental and consists of the first six bars of *God Save the Queen* followed immediately by the first four and last four bars of *O Canada*. The national anthem of Canada is usually played and sung following the "Vice-regal Salute". In the early years of Confederation, both London and Ottawa attempted to prevent the playing of "God Save the Queen" for the Lieutenant-Governor,[10] but soon came to realize that the trappings of the Monarchy have to be accepted in certain instances at the provincial level. In the present day, on some occasions, such as the Remembrance Day Services or in the presence of the Sovereign or other members of the Royal Family, the "Royal Salute", that is, *God Save the Queen,* and the "National Anthem" are both performed.

*Vice-regal Gun Salutes*

By the time Alberta became a province in 1905, permission was granted to fire a 15-gun salute when the Provincial Legislature was opened, "not as a personal honour to the Lieutenant Governor" but rather "as a ceremonial observance emphasizing the importance of the event."[11] Presently, a 15-gun Vice-regal Salute is appropriate on the assembling and closing of a Provincial

Legislature and on an official visit of the Lieutenant-Governor to a saluting station within the officer holder's sphere of jurisdiction, but not more than once in 12 months. Edmonton is the only designated saluting station in Alberta.

(Provincial Archives of Alberta, PA.5233/4)

*Vice-regal Salute*
The 15-gun Vice-regal Salute at the opening of the Alberta Legislature

To celebrate the official birthday of Her Majesty on "Victoria Day" in May, a 21-gun salute is fired on the Legislature grounds and, of course, when Her Majesty visits the provincial capital, she receives a 21-gun salute.

The Lieutenant-Governor's Flag

In addition to these symbols of office, each Lieutenant-Governor possesses an official flag or "standard". The original flag of the Lieutenant-Governor of Alberta was the customary design for most of the Queen's provincial representatives. It consisted of a Union Flag in the centre of which was placed a white disc charged with a shield bearing the 1907 coat of arms of Alberta with a royal crown above it, bordered by a garland of maple leaves.[12]

On 28 September 1981, His Excellency, the Governor General of Canada approved, on behalf of Her Majesty the Queen, a new flag of office for the Lieutenant-Governors.[13] His Honour Frank Lynch-Staunton accepted this new flag for the Lieutenant-Governor of Alberta at Government House.[14] Similar ceremonies were held across the country as eight of the ten Lieutenant-Governors officially received new flags with their provinces' shields centred on a royal blue background. Above the shield is a St. Edward's crown, signifying the sovereign's representative in the province.[15] These flags were redesigned so that the Lieutenant-Governor's flags would correspond with the Governor General's flag which has a royal blue background. The old Lieutenant-Governor's flag for Alberta was placed in the provincial archives.[16]

The Lieutenant-Governor's flag takes precedence over all other flags, except The Queen's Personal Canadian Flag, including the Canadian Flag and the Governor General's Personal Flag when she visits in Alberta. This personal standard of the Lieutenant-Governor is flown at the residence and "from the flagpoles of buildings wherein official duties are carried out." On the death of

### The Lieutenant-Governor's Flag or "Standard"
The flag of the Lieutenant-Governor of Alberta is flown over the office of the Lieutenant-Governor at the main entrance to the Legislature Building

a Lieutenant-Governor, the standard is taken down until a successor is sworn in. Under no circumstances is the Lieutenant-Governor's flag ever flown at half-mast.[17]

This restriction caused a brief gust of controversy to swirl around the flag at the time of the death of Diana, Princess of Wales, on 31 August 1997. As other flags were lowered to half-mast, the question of whether the Lieutenant-Governor's flag should follow suit sent officials scurrying to consult protocol regulations. When His Honour "Bud" Olson learned that the Vice-regal flag could not be flown at half-mast, he had the flag removed from its staff above

44

*Courtesy of the Office of the Lieutenant-Governor of Alberta*

The Flag of the Lieutenant-Governor of Alberta

Photos courtesy of the Office
of the Secretary to the Governor General

Photo Courtesy of Brian Gavriloff, *Edmonton Journal*

## Badge of Service

Lieutenant-Governors and their spouses receive a Vice-regal Badge of Service. The Lieutenant-Governor's Badge is gold and the spouse's Badge is silver. All living and former Lieutenant-Governors and spouses have been given their appropriate Badge. Her Honour Lois Hole wears the Badge at the Opening of the Alberta Legislature.

the main entrance to the Legislature Building. He felt it "'looked disrespectful at the top of the pole.'" His explanation for his actions was that if you cannot find the protocol for unique situations, '"you have to make it up.'"[18]

Lieutenant-Governor's Badge of Office

The most recent symbol authorized to set Lieutenant-Governors apart has been the creation of a Lieutenant-Governor's "Badge of Office". Because males no longer wear the British Civil Dress Uniform, popularly known as the "Windsor uniform" that once clothed the figures of Lieutenant-Governors on special occasions, and because more and more females who have never worn this particular uniform are being appointed to the Office of Lieutenant-Governor, the Vice-regal representatives of Canada's provincial governments can all too easily become nearly indistinguishable from others.[19] The British Civil Dress Uniform consists of "a plumed bicorne (flat, two-sided hat), a gold braided cutaway coat, trousers with a gold braid stripe down the outside of each leg, and a court sword."[20] The last Lieutenant-Governor in Alberta to wear this uniform on official occasions was His Honour Grant MacEwan. The practice changed with His Honour Ralph Steinhauer who found that a "Windsor uniform" cost $3,000 in 1974 and the province was unwilling to supply him with one. Therefore, he wore a "morning suit" except when the government of Peter Lougheed asked him to wear full Indian Chief's regalia for the 1977 Opening of the Legislature to honour the centennial of the signing of the 1877 Treaty Number Seven.[21] A unique Alberta change to the Lieutenant-Governor's wardrobe occurred in 1987. To celebrate the seventy-fifth anniversary of

(City of Edmonton Archives, EA-160-1550)

### British Civil Dress Uniform
His Honour John Bowen wearing the British Civil Dress, or "Windsor" Uniform during Coronation Day celebrations
12 May 1937

(City of Edmonton Archives, EA-10-2664)

### British Civil Dress Uniform
The Honourable John Bowlen wearing the "Windsor" Uniform as he inspects the Guard of Honour at the opening of the Legislature in 1954

(Provincial Archives of Alberta, J.3167/3)

## First Nation Chief's Regalia
Lieutenant-Governor Ralph Steinhauer wore traditional Chief's Regalia at the Opening of the Legislature in 1977

(Jim Cochrane, *The Edmonton Journal*)

## Morning Suit
On 17 April 1996 the newly installed Lieutenant-Governor "Bud" Olson greets the outgoing Lieutenant-Governor Gordon Towers. Both gentlemen wore morning suits, the attire used by male Lieutenant Governors since 1974

Alberta's Legislature Building, the Speaker of the Legislative Assembly, The Honourable David Carter, presented Her Honour Helen Hunley with a robe-of-office on behalf of the Assembly. This cloak has a crown and the original Alberta coat-of-arms on the left breast. Her Honour wore this gift over her dress on ceremonial occasions, such as the opening of a new session of the Legislature or the swearing in of new Members of the Legislative Assembly. No Lieutenant-Governor since Her Honour Helen Hunley has worn this special robe.

Consequently, except on very rare occasions, without any special or official uniforms or robes to set them apart from others, the Sovereign's provincial representatives all too easily blend into the crowd. Consequently, new badges of recognition authorized and designed by the chancellery of the Governor General's office were designed for Lieutenant-Governors to wear in order to signal their importance for their constitutional role and set them apart from others on ceremonial occasions.[22] These badges consist of an attractive ray or star design of four maple leaves, with a central single maple leaf surmounted by a crown.[23]

Along with the badges of recognition, the Lieutenant-Governors have been given the right to bestow special commendation badges to paid or volunteer staff who serve them. There is a limit to the number of awards that can be made during a Lieutenant-Governor's term of service. The commendation badge and pin use the three conjoined leaves found on the arms of the Dominion, surmounted by the crown. Traditionally, direct service to the Crown could be marked by awards of the Royal Victorian Order, but that has been an infrequent mark of honour in Canada.[24]

**Robe of Office**
Her Honour Helen Hunley wears her custom designed Robe of Office as she swears in MLA Ray Martin

(Provincial Archives of Alberta, 95.48/89-08272)

**Formal Gown**
In Alberta, female Lieutenant-Governors have traditionally worn formal gowns such as Her Honour Lois Hole at the New Years' Levee (2002)

(Courtesy of Lt Col Frank Kozar, Edmonton)

Official Residence

Architecture has always played a major symbolic role in establishing the importance and legitimacy of the Crown in Canada. As the noted French novelist Victor Hugo wrote: "the greatest productions of architecture are not so much individual as social works...the deposit left by a people."[25] In other words, structures capture the spirit of an age and represent the aspirations of a people.[26] Because the Crown represents all that is most cherished by a people, it is only natural that Vice-regal architecture should reflect these characteristics back to a society. One of the main physical features of the Crown has been an official residence where the sovereign's representatives may entertain, greet visitors and carry out the responsibilities of the Vice-regal office. At the time Alberta entered Confederation as a province, a magnificent Government House was planned for the Crown's representative at the same time the Legislature was being built. Because the edifice for the people's representatives had priority, the Lieutenant-Governor had to find an appropriate home until work could begin on Government House.

During the first years of Confederation, the province used the home of The Honourable Frank Oliver as the official residence of His Honour, Lieutenant-Governor George Bulyea. This home was located on the south east corner of 103 Street and 100 Avenue in Edmonton. Frank Oliver had built the three storey brick house in 1905, the year he entered the federal cabinet and moved his family to Ottawa. With a commanding view of the river valley, this twelve-room mansion served well as the Lieutenant-Governor's residence until 1913.[27] Many of the most famous functions in the social life of the early years

(City of Edmonton Archives, EB26-347)

*Government House 1905-1913*
The home of the Honourable Frank Oliver served as Government House from 1905 to 1913

of the province were held in this home.[28]

Government House eventually arose on the Groat Estates. The structure was designed by Allan M. Jeffers, the architect of the Legislature and a graduate of the Rhode Island School of Design in the United States.[29] The impressive building which was opened officially on 7 October 1913 was built on a high bluff with a commanding view of the North Saskatchewan River. A magnificent conservatory filled with flowers and tropical plants adjoined this three story mansion. A large stable for the horses and carriages of the Lieutenant-Governor was constructed at the same time. This splendid residence with a steel and concreted frame, covered with sandstone brought from a

(Provincial Archives of Alberta, B.3457)

## Government House 1913
Government House shortly after it was opened

(Glenbow Archives, ND-3-4883a)

## Government House 1929
Lieutenant-Governor and Mrs. Eva Egbert in the garden of Government House (note the Conservatory on the west side of Government House)

Government House 2004

quarry near Calgary, sat on 28 acres of trees and gardens. The two-storey bay windows, mullioned windows and triangular gables are typical of the Jacobethan Revival. Although widely popular throughout North America at this time, the Jacobethan Revival style of Government House is seldom found in Alberta.

The last chatelaine of Government House, Edith Bowen, described it as "homey", but a place of "quality and elegance".[30] It was beautifully furnished with many European pieces. There were antiques, "Queen Anne furniture, rich draperies and carpets, and stocks of crested china, silver services and candlesticks embossed with the crest of the Province of Alberta."[31] The ballroom wing was planned, but never built, because the first resident, His

Honour George Bulyea, did not approve of dancing. A reception hall, drawing room, grand dining room and music room were on the main floor. Visiting dignitaries were quartered on the second floor and the third floor contained the servant's quarters.[32]

### Interior of Government House 1915

(Provincial Archives of Alberta, B.3454)

### The Reception Hall

(Provincial Archives of Alberta, B.3453)

The Dining Room

(Provincial Archives of Alberta, B.3452)

The Library

56

(Provincial Archives of Alberta, A.1976)

**The Study**
The Honourable William Egbert in his study at
Government House (1929)

Government House was to serve the same formal setting for public ceremonies and entertainment as Government House in Ottawa did. The highlight of the social season in Edmonton, the Opening of the Legislature, always had a social aspect which was held at Government House. The event was a very formal white tie affair with all members of the Legislature and their wives invited as well as the President and faculty members of the University, the judiciary, clergy, police, military and the various officers of the Legislature. The Lieutenant-Governor wore his distinguished Windsor uniform and his wife a long evening gown.  Guests were treated to refreshments, alcoholic or non-alcoholic depending on the Lieutenant-Governor, and hors-d'oeuvres in the large Reception Room, the Billiards Room downstairs and the Conservatory at the side of the main structure.

In addition to this yearly ritual, the wife of the Lieutenant-Governor often gave "teas".  Her Honour Eva Egbert gave frequent teas at Government House, often with the wife of the President of the University of Alberta, Annie Tory, pouring.  Annie Tory was a favourite tea pourer in Edmonton because she was equally at home pouring from a professor's brown betty or turning the tap on the huge silver urn at Government House.  More importantly, she kept cups filled while carrying on a running conversation.  Once, however, disaster struck.  At one of Her Honour's teas, the worst possible scenario occurred.  In the small privileged society of Edmonton, Her Honour Eva Egbert, Annie Tory and the wife of a professor at the university, all showed up in the same dress! It was as if the women's fashion store where the three identical dresses were bought had set out deliberately to sabotage this charming social occasion.  All was not unpleasant as the three startled women separated themselves in different parts of the imposing mansion throughout the social.  The morning after this unhappy event, the Government House chauffeur took all three dresses back to where they had been purchased and secured refunds without any hassle![33]

The Lieutenant-Governor's wife entertained many women's clubs such as the Women's Institutes, the Imperial Order of the Daughters of the Empire, the Women's Canadian Club and the Victorian Order of Nurses at Government House.  During the Christmas season, the tradition developed that the Boys

**Entertaining at Government House**
His Honour William Egbert with children

*Garden Party at Government House*
His Honour George Bulyea hosts a reception for Lord Strathcona
7 September 1909

Choir from All Saints Cathedral would come to Government House to sing Christmas carols under the direction of Vernon Barford. Her Honour Edith Bowen explained that the boys enjoyed their visit and spent most of the evening riding up and down on the elevator![34] In summer, the gardens surrounding the House were beautiful and garden parties were held. One of the last garden parties before the house was closed was for the visiting Canadian Governor General and his wife, Lord and Lady Tweedsmuir. A marquee was erected where the Lieutenant-Governor and his wife greeted their guests and introduced them to their Excellencies.

Because the conclusion of the First World War brought financial restraints by governments, some small-minded politicians began to question the cost of maintaining Government House. In 1925, a back-bencher with the United Farmers of Alberta government not only questioned the usefulness of the Lieutenant-Governor's mansion, but the office itself, and proposed to close Government House and abolish the position of the Queen's representative in Alberta. The mansion was put on the market, but with only one bid, the motion which had passed the Legislature was rescinded and the mansion received a well-deserved reprieve from the pettiness of foolish politicians. Nevertheless, unease continued over the building as Lieutenant-Governors put in requests for maintenance funding. By 1927 new draperies were required and His Honour William Egbert felt he needed a new victrola. Again in 1931, draperies were worn out and replaced, but Premier Brownlee refused to provde His Honour William Walsh with a grand fireplace for the reception hall.[35] Then came the government of William Aberhart. In an act of malice and with total lack of foresight, William Aberhart made certain His Honour was ousted from the official residence in May 1938.

William Aberhart was angered that the Lieutenant-Governor had "reserved" Social Credit legislation and had asked for Ottawa's guidance on the matter. As a response to the Lieutenant-Governor's actions, Aberhart challenged the "reserve" power of the Lieutenant-Governor before the courts, but the Supreme Court found that the power of reservation existed and was "subject to no limitation or restriction."[36] Aberhart was thus forced to act in other, constitutional, though questionable, ways. The first public indication of what Aberhart proposed as punishment for His Honour came in December at a Social Credit Convention. There, delegates voted to stop all provincial funding for the maintenance of the Lieutenant-Governor and for his official residence, Government House. Then in March 1938, the Alberta Legislature, sitting in committee of supply, instructed the government not to spend any monies for the maintenance of Government House and the Lieutenant-Governor. Existing monies for these purposes expired at the end of March 1938. Since the federal government only pays for the salary of the Lieutenant-Governor, His Honour faced problems with respect to accommodation and staff. Nevertheless, he chose to ignore the Legislature's actions and became very circumspect about where he placed his signature.

As the end of March approached and the Sovereign's representative gave no indication he intended to move or fire his staff, the government gave him one month's grace and expenditures were carried out by special warrant, signed appropriately by His Honour. As the end of April approached, the battle lines between the Lieutenant-Governor and the Social Credit government became clearer. Bowen claimed that he could vacate Government House only through "proper procedure" which for him meant by an Order-in-Council which he as Lieutenant-Governor would have to sign. The government, on the other hand, argued that an Order-in-Council was not necessary to close a building owned by the provincial government.[37] There the matter rested as 12 midnight arrived on 30 April. A stand-off existed!

Even though the government issued orders to cut off all utilities, including water, lights, telephone and gas on 30 April, the Lieutenant-Governor, his wife and staff remained held up in Government House. As the crisis deepened, the government decided on a new course of action. All staff, including caretaker and secretary were released from service and all supplies of office were cut off.[38] Aberhart decided to grant Bowen another temporary extension of residence and to postpone the cutting off of utilities.[39] However, this action was not swift enough for the city's telephone company which had already cut the telephones. By oversight, one telephone in the basement of the residence formerly used by the now released caretaker, remained functional. Fortunately for His Honour, the water, light and gas companies were less efficient and the orders to terminate service were canceled in time.

His Honour, ill with the flu, and his wife remained dignified refugees in the elegant setting of Government House, awaiting the deadline of the 10 day extension. During this period, ordinary Albertans came to the Vice-regal door in anger and many others sent threatening letters. People were suffering the stress and strain of the Depression and felt the Lieutenant-Governor was somehow a barrier to the good life which the Social Credit Premier, William Aberhart, had promised. The Lieutenant-Governor's wife described this period as "frightening".[40] On Friday afternoon, 6 May 1938, His Honour finally signed an Order-in-Council formally closing Government House on 10 May.[41] Just before the deadline, at 9 PM Monday evening 9 May, the Vice-regal couple left Government House for a federally run place of refuge, the Hotel Macdonald. There they took up residence in a fifth floor suite and hung the Union Jack on the flagpole to signify their presence.

In response to the Canadian Prime Minister's call that the Crown be supplied with "essential services",[42] the government eventually allowed His Honour to phone for a ride if he required transportation on official business. They refused His Honour's request for an office other than the one in the Legislature Building,[43] the permanent use of a car and chauffeur, secretary and supplies.[44] Despite the intervention of the Canadian Prime Minister, Mackenzie King, on behalf of the Lieutenant-Governor who considered the Aberhart government's actions as disloyalty to the Crown, the Premier refused to relent and forced the Lieutenant-Governor to use taxis and the secretarial pool to meet his needs.[45] The government took an inventory of all furnishings in Government House,[46] and then auctioned them off.

It was not clear at the time whether the action by the Legislature in cutting all maintenance costs for the structure would result in the decision being overturned as in 1925. As time passed, however, it became clear that the rash decision of 1938 would remain in place.[47] News of the closing of Government House swept through the media and reached the desk of the

(Provincial Archives of Alberta, B1.252/3)

Lieutenant-Governor's Office in the Legislature Building
1926

(Courtesy of Lt Col Frank Kozar, Edmonton)

Lieutenant-Governor's Office in Legislature Building
1999
His Honour Bud Olson held a reception in his office for Canadian Legion Members following the presentation of poppies before Remembrance Day

King. When King George VI and Queen Elizabeth arrived for their visit to Edmonton in 1939, the King asked the Lieutenant-Governor at the station whether they were going to pass by Government House?[48] Because the Lieutenant-Governor and his wife had no official residence, a reception for the King and Queen was held in the Legislative Assembly Chamber and then a smaller one followed in the Lieutenant-Governor's suite of offices in the Legislature Building.

The forlorn looking Government House remained vacant until 1942 when it was leased to North West Airlines Incorporated and used by American forces building the Alaska highway. When the Governor General, the Earl of Athlone and Princess Alice visited Edmonton just after the war, Princess Alice expressed her displeasure that the government had not restored Government House; she talked to the Premier's wife about the matter. She wondered how Edith Bowen and her husband could carry out their duties properly without such a home.[49] Nothing came of this royal intervention. After 1950, the federal Department of Veterans Affairs bought the building and it became a home for disabled veterans.

Government House and the property surrounding it were returned to the province and in 1967 the Provincial Museum and Archives of Alberta opened on the site. Renovations proceeded with Government House and the conservatory was demolished. No longer suitable as an official residence for the Lieutenant-Governor because of its lack of privacy, it was reserved for state entertaining and conferences. During 1975 and 1976, Government House underwent a complete refurbishing under Premier Lougheed's guidance. At the end of this process, the Premier's wife, Jeanne, proudly proclaimed that the tired floors which once groaned with dry-rot were "replaced with a carpet so plush a footprint stay[ed] in it for an hour."[50] Presently, there is a large combination reception and dining area on the main floor, as well as a music room and a library. The second floor consists of a central reception area surrounded by six small conference rooms, each named after one of the six Lieutenant-Governors who had lived in Government House. The third floor houses a large conference facility named the Alberta Room. At the time Government House was reopened in August 1976, Premier Lougheed said that such an official "Government House" was required for a province like Alberta which was climbing to a place of power within Confederation.[51] Thus today, Government House stands restored, but not the home of the Lieutenant-Governor; it remains elegant and stately but crippled as a symbol of the Crown's presence in Alberta.

When Lieutenant-Governor Bowen was expelled from Government House in 1938, he moved first to a suite of rooms in the Hotel Macdonald and then to rented quarters at #45 St. George's Crescent, the home of a federal cabinet minister, the Honourable James Mckinnon. The crescent, named for the patron saint of England, wends its way along Ramsey Ravine to the north bank of the North Saskatchewan River. From 1938 until 1947 Lieutenant-Governor Bowen lived in the home.[52] The Bowen's attempted to carry out the same functions they had undertaken at Government House, but in a modified form because of their smaller home. Just before he left office, His Honour bought a home at 10226 Connaught Drive where he resided until his death.

The next two Lieutenant-Governors lived in their own homes. The Honourable John Bowlen built a house in Edmonton at 13604 Ravine Drive and the Honourable C. Percy Page remained in the home he had built in Edmonton at 10312-133 Street(Alexander Crescent).[53] Clearly, after 1938, architecturally, the presence of the Lieutenant-Governor had diminished!

As this awkward reality festered in the public mind, the Alberta government was finally shamed into corrective action and bought an official residence for the Lieutenant-Governor in 1966. This mea culpa by the government occurred at the time His Honour Grant MacEwan was installed into office. The first thing the Calgarian, Grant MacEwan, had to do after being sworn into office that year was go house hunting. The MacEwan's purchased a bungalow at 13845 MacKinnon Ravine while a controversy raged over the provincial government's insensitivity to the Lieutenant-Governor's housing requirements. At one point the City of Calgary threatened to purchase a home for the MacEwans if the province refused.[54] The Ernest Manning government was so embarrassed by the lack of any accommodation for the Vice-regal couple that the provincial government bought a bungalow at 58 St. George's Crescent in the Glenora district as the new official residence of the Crown's representative in Alberta.[55] This long, low-slung cedar bungalow stretched across three lots and was an outstanding example of leading edge architecture of the days after World War II. The eminent Edmonton architect, John Rule, designed this home which was constructed in 1950 with a fieldstone fireplace and low-pitched roof.[56] There were eight rooms in the home with a capacity to seat twelve guests at dinner or hold a reception for eighty-five people. One

(John Lucas, *The Edmonton Journal*)

## Official Residence
The Lieutenant-Governor's official residence at 58 St. George's Crescent
(This residence was demolished in 2004)

member of staff was assigned to the residence and the grounds were maintained by the appropriate provincial government department. The MacEwan's lived in their own newly purchased home for one year while renovations were completed on the new "official residence" of the Lieutenant-Governor.[57] This residence lacked the dignity of Government House and one Lieutenant-Governor who lived in it, His Honour Frank Lynch-Staunton, is on record as not liking it.[58] Nevertheless, when the government of Premier Ralph Klein decided to tear down the residence 25 March 2004, Paula Simons of the *Edmonton Journal* blamed the government for a "pretty lousy job of looking after our property." She contended that "So little maintenance and repair has been done to the house over the past 20 years that it has almost reached the point where it is a virtual write-off."[59] Simons wondered aloud in the press about how little regard the Alberta government must hold the Queen to

## Interior of Residence at 58 St. George's Crescent

(Provincial Archives of Alberta, A13372)

**Television Room**

(Provincial Archives of Alberta, A13370)

**Living Room**

(Provincial Archives of Alberta, A13368)

**Living Room Looking Towards Dining Room**

"neglect and ruin her representative's house, then knock it down and sell off a third of the property without telling anyone and with no definite plans to rebuild or replace it".[60] By June 2004, one lot of the property formerly set aside for the Lieutenant-Governor's residence was listed at $849,000; despite Premier Klein's insistence that "'We're building a new place'", no plans were afoot to build a new residence on the remainder of the lots on St. George's Crescent.[61] Whatever the merits of the Vice-regal residence, "On the eve of Alberta's centennial the lieutenant-governor's residence was demolished because the cost of repairs exceeded its value."[62] Yet again, Alberta's Lieutenant-Governor was without a residence despite the grant of $5.3 million, made in the spring of 2003, to restore "Beaulieu", the Lougheed family mansion in Calgary![63]

Because of the importance of Calgary in the province, the government re-fitted the McDougall School, named after the famous missionary family, to house offices for the use of the Lieutenant-Governor and government officials while in Calgary.[64] Her Honour Helen Hunley opened the renovated building on Tuesday, 8 September 1987.[65] Basically, this McDougall Centre serves as Government House "South".

Someday, the architectural symbol of the Crown might be restored, and a building of grandeur to match the original Government House might be built to symbolize the importance of the Office of Lieutenant-Governor to Alberta.[66]

Transportation

Besides losing an official residence in the twenty-first century, the manner of transportation has relied on functionality, rather than elevate the monarchy's Alberta representative within society. In the present age, there has been nothing particularly romantic or splendid about the way the Lieutenant-Governor has travelled. In earlier times, the Lieutenant-Governor rode in an open, horse-drawn carriage with an escort of Mounted Police or military in attendance on ceremonial occasions. More recently, a chauffeur-driven limousine has been used. There is a fixture located on the right side of the front bumper of the vehicle for mounting a miniature version of the Lieutenant-Governor's standard.[67] The license plate for the Lieutenant-Governor's automobile is stamped "LT GOV" followed by the current year.

(Glenbow Archives, NC-6-1660)

*Carriage*
Lieutenant-Governor Brett using carriage at the Opening of the Legislature
1916

72

(Glenbow Archives, NA-2005-1)

## Automobile
The Prince of Whales and Lieutenant-Governor Brett in an automobile in front of the Palliser Hotel at Calgary, 14 September 1919

## Automobile
His Honour Percy Page and his chauffeur standing in front of his official car, November 1960
(Note the year "1960" on the licence plate)

(Provincial Archives of Alberta, PA.674/4)

The placing of miniature flag on the car and the unique license plate which alone distinguish the Lieutenant-Governor's mode of transportation from any other vehicle on the road, have not prevented the Lieutenant-Governor from facing embarrassing situations involving transportation. In 1944 a metal shortage almost caused the Lieutenant-Governor to lose his license plate-year tie! For the first time in the thirty years since motor licenses were issued in Alberta, the number of the Lieutenant-Governor's license did not correspond to the year. The province had decided to adopt a sticker system whereby all car owners would keep their previous year's plates and attach a sticker to the windshield and rear window in place of 1944 license plates. Consequently, a "1944 plate" was issued to George Langland who remarked that "It's too bad a chauffeur doesn't go with the plate."[68] Fortunately, the Lieutenant-Governor's chauffeur, James Marskell, was a born diplomat who got together with George Langland, a most reasonable chap and following their conversation, Langland offered to hand over his 1944 plate to the Lieutenant-Governor in return for receiving His Honour's 1943 plates with stickers. Broad-minded provincial licensing authorities authorized the transfer, thereby preserving a longstanding Alberta tradition![69]

His Honour Ralph Steinhauer experienced a memorable time when his limousine ran out of gasoline and he had to hitch a ride back to Edmonton. His chauffeur flagged down a passing car and the Lieutenant-Governor's vehicle was left by the roadside. The "good Samaritan" drove His Honour to his residence and left the chauffeur looking for fuel. Meanwhile, a Mountie happened along and found the abandoned Lieutenant-Governor's limousine. There were some anxious moments when the Mountie radioed in an alert that His Honour had been kidnapped.[70] Clearly the modern means of transportation is not always the most reliable.

    A frightening road rage incident shook the driver of Her Honour Lois Hole's official black Lexus sedan on 9 October 2002. When returning to the Legislature from an official event in Spruce Grove, Alberta, Her Honour's driver noticed a yellow and brown pickup truck pulling out of an alley in front of the Vice-regal car. Thinking the truck was not going to stop, Her Honour's chauffeur swerved left and braked. The driver of the truck pulled out in front and slammed on his brakes. He threw the truck into reverse, spun his wheels so much that his tires smoked and backed up towards the stopped Vice-regal car as if trying to ram it. Her Honour's driver was forced to back up for three blocks. The truck driver pursued Her Honour's vehicle down roads and an alley before Her Honour's driver was able to escape and arrive safely at Her Honour's Legislature Office. The truck driver who was not taking his medication for his manic-depressive disorder at the time, later apologized in court and said he was just "playing a little game with the black car...."[71] Her Honour's shaken staff came to realize through this experience that even an official vehicle is not necessarily the safest means of Vice-regal transportation.

    At times in this democratic and functional age, the ceremonial presentation of the unifying symbol of the Lieutenant-Governor becomes necessary through the preservation of some anachronisms such as the use of a landau on special occasions.[72] For certain state ceremonials such as the

Installation of a Lieutenant-Governor or the Opening of the Alberta Legislature, the Lieutenant-Governor has the option of choosing to ride in an open landau or an automobile. Sadly, more often than not, the preferred method of transportation for the Vice-Regal party today is the automobile and aircraft. Possibly this decision is made because the Opening of the Legislature generally occurs in bitterly cold February weather; however, an open landau could be used for Her Honour's arrival for ceremonies on the Legislature grounds to celebrate the Queen's official birthday on Victoria Day or Canada Day functions on 1 July.

Besides these very concrete symbols of office, there are other awards and positions which only a Lieutenant-Governor receives or occupies which symbolize the Vice-regal representation in the province of Alberta. One of these positions is Chancellor of the Order of Excellence of Alberta.

Chancellor of the Order of Excellence

Since the Crown is the font of all honours in Canada and represents our highest ideals, it is only right that honours should be given individuals in the province to remind Albertans of the things we cherish. Therefore, awards are given to individuals and affect their status within the community, a status which the people through the Crown value and recognize. In 1979, the Alberta Order of Excellence was established by the Peter Lougheed government to "give recognition to Albertans who have rendered service of the highest distinction and singular excellence for and on behalf of the residents of Alberta."[73] His Honour Ralph Steinhauer was consulted about this Order before he left office and enthusiastically endorsed the proposal.[74] The Lieutenant-Governor of Alberta became the Chancellor of the Order. Because the bill establishing the Order was given Royal Assent on 16 November 1979,[75] the first Chancellor was His Honour Frank Lynch-Staunton. Following provisions set out in the Act, the Lieutenant-Governor by Order-In-Council prescribed the seal, motto and insignia of the Order. The first investiture was then held in 1981 with the Honourable Ernest Manning as the first recipient of the honour. "Members of the Order are entitled to use the initials A.O.E. after their names."[76]

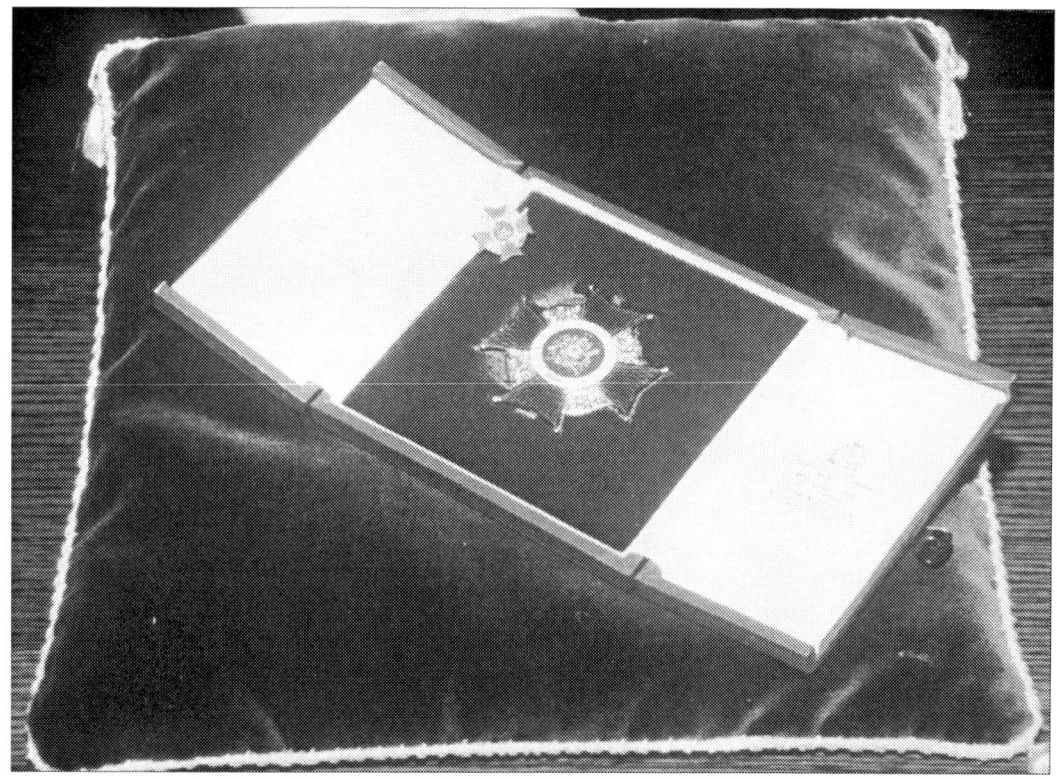

(Provincial Archives of Alberta, 96.258/9130153)

*Medallion of the Order of Excellence of Alberta*

The insignia of the Alberta Order of Excellence "consists of a silver, gilt and enamel medallion attached to a ribbon distinctive to the province."[77] The medallion along with a miniature of the insignia design is presented to Members at a ceremony at Government House. The gold detail on the four arms of the medallion represents prairie wheat, the roses portray the floral emblem of the province and the Coat of Arms is contained in the central circle. The Order of Excellence is the highest honour that can be bestowed on an Albertan by the Lieutenant-Governor.

Vice-Prior of the Most Venerable Order Of St John Of Jerusalem

In addition to serving as Chancellor of the Alberta Order of Excellence, since 1949, Lieutenant-Governors have been admitted to the Order of St John of Jerusalem in the province of Alberta.[78] The Canadian Prime Minister in 1934, the Right Honourable R. B. Bennett, favoured the use of British titles as a legitimate form of compensation as honours for Canadians and allowed this Order to admit representatives of the Crown. However, the Lieutenant-Governor who was serving at the time, His Honour William Walsh, was not admitted to the Order while others such as the Governor General and the Ontario Lieutenant-Governor were admitted to the Order.[79] As of 25 October 1990, the Most Venerable Order of the Hospital of St John of Jerusalem has been reinstated as a Canadian Order. The Sovereign Head of the Order is Queen Elizabeth II and the Governor General is the Prior for Canada. Initially, all Lieutenant-Governors were invested into the Order as Knights or Dames of Grace and reclassified if they became armigerous (obtained a personal coat of arms). The spouses of Lieutenant-Governors were admitted to the Order as Officers and they continue to be admitted to the Order currently at this grade. Upon assuming the office, the Lieutenant-Governor has the right to choose to be admitted to this Order in Alberta or Ottawa. The Lieutenant-Governor also becomes Vice-Prior of the Order for Alberta.

As Vice-Priors or Head of the Order of St John for Alberta, the Lieutenant-Governor presides over the annual Investitures in Alberta and confers the rank and insignia for each grade of the Order (Serving Member, Officer, Commander and Knight/Dame). As well, the Vice-Prior in Alberta confers Lifesaving Medals of the Order (Gold, Silver and Bronze) and the Service Medal of the Order (representing 12 years of service to the Order). The Vice-Prior may attend annual general meetings of the St John Ambulance, although in the last quarter century, no Vice-Prior has attended an Alberta Council Annual General Meeting.

Shortly after His Honour "Bud" Olson was admitted to the Order, it was observed that the Government of Canada assisted Lieutenant-Governors in becoming armigerous during their term of office. This procedure resulted in admitting them to the Order as a Knight or Dame of Grace and in a short period of time, having to reclassify them as Knights and Dames of Justice. This practice became expensive as sets of insignia are given to the Lieutenant-Governors. The Order Committee then decided to award Knight and Dame of Justice insignia at the outset of each Vice-regal term to save time and expense.

The Order of St John of Jerusalem was originally a military-religious order, founded in the eleventh century to provide medical help to the crusaders in its hospital in Jerusalem. Named after St John the Baptist, the Order was dissolved in England by King Henry VIII, but revived in Britain in the nineteenth century. A royal charter was granted in 1888 which established the Order of the Hospital of St John of Jerusalem as a British Order of Chivalry, with Queen Victoria as its head. The modern Order continues humanitarian tasks in several parts of the world.

Beginning in 1948, investitures for the Order of St John were held in Alberta. On Saturday, 17 September 1949, the decoration of Knight of Grace, the highest rank of the Order, was conferred on the Honourable John Bowen by C.A. Gray of Ottawa, the Sub-Prior of the Order who travelled to Alberta to represent His Excellency Viscount Alexander who was the Governor General. Since His Honour was indisposed, he did not attend the pubic investiture in the Legislative Chamber, but rather had his investiture in private.[80] On Monday 23 November 1953, His Honour John Bowlen received the highest rank of the Order in the Lieutenant-Governor's Legislature offices before proceeding to the Legislative Chamber for the investiture of other members of the Order in Alberta.[81] With the exception of His Honour Grant MacEwan who was never admitted to the Order and His Honour Ralph Steinhauer, all Lieutenant-Governors until the investiture of His Honour Gordon Towers, travelled to Ottawa to be admitted to the Order. Since Gordon Towers, all ceremonies have taken place in Alberta. His Honour Percy Page was invested as a Knight of Grace of the Order of St John of Jerusalem in Ottawa on 30 October 1964 by Governor General Georges Vanier.[82]

Her Honour Helen Hunley was invested as a Dame of the Order of St John of Jerusalem at a ceremony at Notre Dame Basilica in Ottawa. Her Excellency, Governor General Jeanne Sauvé presided over this investiture. Her word proved greater than the sword on this occasion. Madame Sauvé is said to have been indignant when told that males would receive the traditional treatment of a tap on the shoulder with a sword when they were dubbed Knights of St John while females would just receive three taps of the hand on a shoulder when becoming Dames of the Order. In the end, all individuals, whether male or female, invested into the Order at the same time as Her Honour Helen Hunley, received three simple taps of the hand on a shoulder.[83]

(Courtesy of Lt Col Frank Kozar, Edmonton)

### Venerable Order of St John of Jerusalem
Her Honour Lois Hole admitted as Dame of the Venerable Order of St John of Jerusalem, 9 June 2000 at St. Albert, Alberta

In Alberta, the last Lieutenant-Governor to be inducted into the Order was Her Honour Lois Hole who became a Dame of Justice on 9 June 2000 at a ceremony in St. Albert, the Lieutenant-Governor's home town. In addition to this investiture, Her Honour Lois Hole, like her predecessors, also received an Honourary degree from the University of Alberta.

University Of Alberta Visitor and LLD Degrees

Since Alberta joined Confederation as a province, all Lieutenant-Governors have been granted Honourary doctoral degrees from the University of Alberta except His Honour Philip Primrose who was in office less than one year and thus the university was unable to confer a degree upon him before his untimely death.[84] The University of Alberta made a policy decision from the

(City of Edmonton Archives, EA-10-2663)

*Honourary Degree*
His Honour John Bowlen receiving an Honourary Degree
(LLD) from the University of Alberta, 15 May 1952

(Courtesy of the University of Alberta)

*Honourary Degree*
His Honour Bud Olson receiving his Honourary Degree (LLD) from the University of Alberta, 20 November 1996

outset of its existence to grant an honourary degree to Lieutenant-Governors and His Honour George Bulyea enjoyed the distinction of receiving the first honourary degree the university ever awarded. Her Honour Lois Hole was the last Lieutenant-Governor to receive an Honourary Degree (always Honourary Doctor of Laws degree) at the fall convocation of the University of Alberta in 2000 just a few months after assuming her Vice-regal office.

The relationship between the Lieutenant-Governor and the University of Alberta has always been very close. One of the first Acts of the Alberta Legislature was to establish and incorporate a university for the province. Article 4 of the Act of 1906 made the Lieutenant-Governor "the visitor of the university".[85] Visitor "is a person who officially visits an institution for the purpose of inspection or supervision in order to prevent or remove abuses or

*Lieutenant-Governor as Visitor to the University of Alberta*
As Visitor to the University of Alberta, His Honour William Walsh (seated) observes the Honourable Frank Oliver receive an honourary degree at the University of Alberta Convocation Ceremony, 14 May 1931

irregularities."[86] The Visitor at a university follows an old British tradition which made an individual of high rank or eminence as the highest authority and court of last appeal for a university. This post existed for seventy years until, in 1976, the government amended the Universities Act and abolished the "office of Visitor".[87] This action resulted from an internal dispute over tenure within the University of Alberta which drew the Lieutenant-Governor, as Visitor, into an untenable "political matter" which could only be addressed by having the role of Visitor abolished.

The case involved a professor, Dr. Anthony Vanek, who was hired to teach in the Department of Slavic languages. In 1972 he was denied tenure by the Faculty of Arts. When his appeal within the "normal" university structure did not overturn his dismissal, he appealed to "the Visitor" of the University, the Lieutenant-Governor, asking him to overturn the decision of the university tenure appeal committee. Much to the chagrin of the Lieutenant-Governor, Dr. Vanek's solicitor focused attention on the Visitor's function in the resolution of university disputes.[88] Because this appeal could cast the Lieutenant-Governor in a role which could bring disrepute to the Crown, the Lieutenant-Governor asked the Legislature to abolish the post and it complied in November 1976.[89]

The question then turned on whether the Visitor's jurisdiction still applied to the Vanek case or was the office of Visitor retroactively abolished? In order to help resolve this conflict, Vanek won a hearing in the fall of 1976, by order of the Visitor, which re-constituted virtually the same tenure committee as previously entertained his case. In January 1977, it recommended that Vanek be granted a two-year contract.[90] The Board of Governors of the University, however, turned down this recommendation and refused to hire Vanek for any period.[91] In the end, Vanek sued the university and an out-of-court settlement was reached. The honour of His Honour had been spared but the post of Visitor was abolished!

Despite the loss of the position of "Visitor", the Lieutenant-Governors continue to receive Honourary degrees from the University of Alberta and at the request of the Senate and by the custom of the University, the Lieutenant-Governor administers the oath of office to all Chancellors.[92] This tradition remains one that is cherished by both the University of Alberta and the province's Lieutenant-Governors.

(Courtesy of the University of Alberta)

*Lieutenant-Governor Administering the Oath of Office*
Her Honour Lois Hole administering the Oath of Office to the new Chancellor of the University of Alberta, John Ferguson, at convocation 14 June 2000

Through these various symbols of office, the Lieutenant-Governor embodies those characteristics which Albertans' cherish and hope to emulate. Through their use and preservation, they remind Albertans of their highest ideals and act as an inspiration through which the people of the province derive special meaning. In this way, the Lieutenant-Governor perpetuates the honour of the Crown.

## NOTES

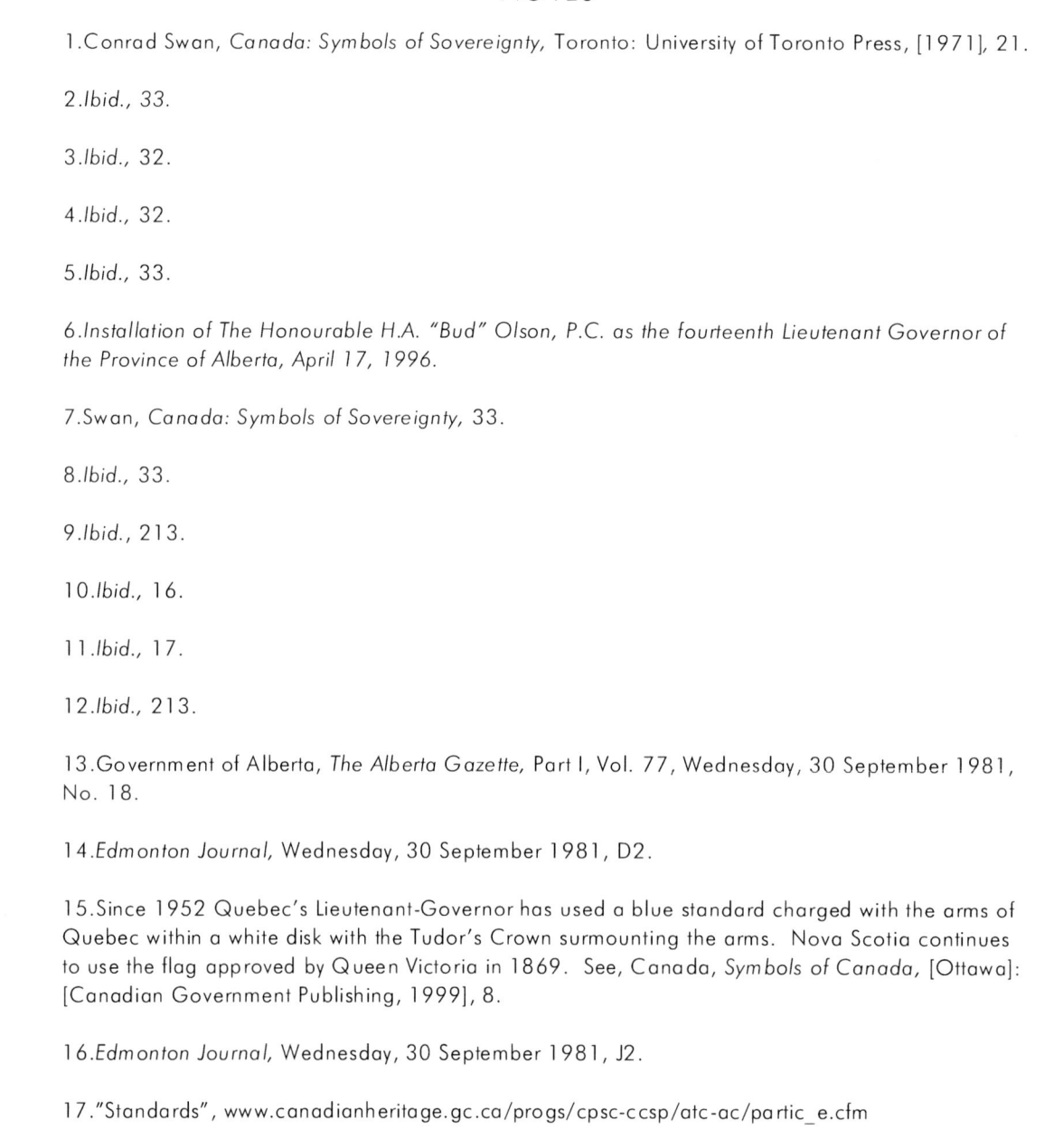

1. Conrad Swan, *Canada: Symbols of Sovereignty,* Toronto: University of Toronto Press, [1971], 21.

2. *Ibid.,* 33.

3. *Ibid.,* 32.

4. *Ibid.,* 32.

5. *Ibid.,* 33.

6. *Installation of The Honourable H.A. "Bud" Olson, P.C. as the fourteenth Lieutenant Governor of the Province of Alberta, April 17, 1996.*

7. Swan, *Canada: Symbols of Sovereignty,* 33.

8. *Ibid.,* 33.

9. *Ibid.,* 213.

10. *Ibid.,* 16.

11. *Ibid.,* 17.

12. *Ibid.,* 213.

13. Government of Alberta, *The Alberta Gazette,* Part I, Vol. 77, Wednesday, 30 September 1981, No. 18.

14. *Edmonton Journal,* Wednesday, 30 September 1981, D2.

15. Since 1952 Quebec's Lieutenant-Governor has used a blue standard charged with the arms of Quebec within a white disk with the Tudor's Crown surmounting the arms. Nova Scotia continues to use the flag approved by Queen Victoria in 1869. See, Canada, *Symbols of Canada,* [Ottawa]: [Canadian Government Publishing, 1999], 8.

16. *Edmonton Journal,* Wednesday, 30 September 1981, J2.

17. "Standards", www.canadianheritage.gc.ca/progs/cpsc-ccsp/atc-ac/partic_e.cfm

18. Brian Brennan, *Scoundrels and Scallywags: Characters from Alberta's Past,* [Calgary]: Fifth House, [2002], 184.

19. When the Honourable Iona Campagnolo became British Columbia's Lieutenant-Governor in September 2001, she had a unique Vice-regal uniform designed, "one that would not only be more appropriate for a woman holding office, but would reflect the unique character of the Province of British Columbia". Her Honour now wears this Vice-regal uniform proudly on major state occasions. (See "The Windsor Uniform" www.ltgov.bc/office/uniform.htm

20. D. Blake McDougall, John E. McDonough and Kenneth W. Tingley, *Lieutenant-Governors of the Northwest Territories and Alberta 1876-1991*, Edmonton: Alberta Legislature Library, 1991, 99.

21. His Honour Ralph Steinhauer to His Honour Gorden L. Bennett, Lieutenant-Governor of Prince Edward Island, 13 June 1977, *Provincial Archives of Alberta*, GS Correspondence between Lieutenant-Governors, L-2 "Lieutenant-Governors of Other Provinces", 79.338 Box 9.

22. *The National Post,* Saturday, 17 February 2001.

23. *Ibid.*

24. *Ibid.*

25. Victor Hugo, *The Hunchback of Notre Dame,* New York: [Random House], [1941], 96.

26. *Ibid.,* 116-117.

27. *Edmonton Journal,* 16 May 1957, 1.

28. *Edmonton Bulletin,* 10 June 1943, 16.

29. D.R. Babcock, *A Gentleman of Strathcona, Alexander Cameron Rutherford,* [Calgary]: The Friends of Rutherford House and The University of Calgary Press, [1989], 172.

30. Provincial Archives of Alberta, recorded conversation with Mrs. J. C. (Oliver) Bowen on 27 March 1972, #72.128.

31. Lori Yanish and Shirley Lowe, *Edmonton's West Side Story: The history of the original West End of Edmonton from 1870,* [Edmonton: Jasper Printing Group, 1991], 96.

32. *Ibid.,* 96.

33. Helen Boyd, "Growing up privileged in Edmonton", *Alberta History,* 30.1 (Winter 1982), 10.

34. *Ibid.*

35. *Ibid.,* 97-98.

36. John T. Saywell, "The Lieutenant-Governors", in *The Provincial Political Systems*, comparative essays, eds. David J. Bellamy, Jon H. Pammett and Donald C. Rowat, Toronto: Metheun, [1976],307.

37. *Edmonton Bulletin,* 4 May 1938, 1&2.

38. *Edmonton Journal,* 4 May 1938, 1.

39. *Edmonton Bulletin,* 4 May 1938, 1.

40. Provincial Archives of Alberta, recorded interview with Mrs. J. C. (Oliver) Bowen 27 March 1972, #72.128.

41. *Edmonton Bulletin,* Saturday, 7 May 1938, 1 & 2.

42. *Edmonton Bulletin,* Tuesday, 10 May 1938, 1 & 2.

43. *Edmonton Journal,* Monday 2 May 1938, 2; and 16 May 1938, 1.

44. *Edmonton Bulletin,* Monday, 9 May 1938, 1.

45. David R. Elliott and Iris Miller, *Bible Bill: A Biography of William Aberhart,* [Edmonton]: Reidmore Books, [1987], 278.

46. *Edmonton Bulletin,* 18 May 1938, 1.

47. *Edmonton Journal,* Monday, 9 May 1938. (Editorial)

48. *Ibid.*

49. *Ibid.*

50. *Edmonton Journal,* 4 August 1976, 5.

51. *Edmonton Journal,* 3 August 1976, 19.

52. Edmonton *Real Estate Weekly,* 25 July 2001, 4.

53. *Edmonton Journal,* 20 January 1965.

54. Donna von Hauff, *Everyone's Grandfather: The Life & Times of Grant MacEwan,* Edmonton]: [Grant MacEwan Copmmunity College Foundation/Quon Editions], [1994], 148.

55. *Edmonton Journal,* 8 January 1966 and 16 February 1966.

56. Heritage Canada Foundation, "Heritage Canada calls for the preservation of the Lieutenant-Governor's Official Residence in Edmonton, Alberta", *Canada NewsWire,* Ottawa, 25 February 2004, 1.

57. A photograph and very good detailed description of the Official Residence as it was in 1985 can be found in the *Edmonton Journal,* 1 December 1985.

58. Frank Lynch-Staunton, *Greener Pastures: The Memoirs of F. Lynch-Staunton,* Edmonton: Jasper Printing Group, 1987, 46.

59. *Edmonton Journal,* Thursday, 12 February 2004, B1.

60. *Edmonton Journal,* Thursday, 12 February 2004, B1.

61. *Edmonton Journal,* Tuesday, 1 June 2004, B2.

62. Ellen Ireland, Letter to the Editor, *Edmonton Journal,* Thursday, 1 April 2004, A19.

63. *Edmonton Journal,* Thursday, 12 February 2004, B1.

64. *Calgary Herald,* 6 September 1987.

65. *Calgary Herald,* 6 September 1987.

66. Some have suggested that a residence in the ornate Beaux-arts style on the site of the present Terrace Building on the Alberta Legislature grounds would be most fitting for Alberta's Lieutenant-Governor.

67. D. Blake McDougall, John E. McDonough and Kenneth W. Tingley, *Lieutenant-Governors of the Northwest Territories and Alberta 1876-1991,* Edmonton: Alberta Legislative Library, 1991, 103.

68. *Edmonton Journal,* 8 March 1944.

69. *Edmonton Journal,* 28 March 1944.

70. *Globe and Mail,* 18 July 1979.

71. *Edmonton Journal,* Thursday, 13 February 2003, A1 & A20.

72. David Cannadine, "The context, performance and meaning of ritual: The British Monarchy and the 'Invention of Tradition', c. 1820-1977", in Eric Hobsbawm and Terence Ranger, eds., *The Invention of Tradition,* Cambridge: University of Cambridge Press, 1992, 111-112 & 118.

73. Government of Alberta, *Alberta Hansard,* (Mary Le Messurier) 19 October 1979, 863.

74. *Ibid.,* 1107.

75. Government of Alberta, *Alberta Hansard,* 16 November 1979,

76. *Symbols of Canada,* [Ottawa: Department of Canadian Heritage, 1999], 47.

77. *Ibid.*

78. There are those who claim that His Honour William Walsh was the first Lieutenant-Governor to be admitted to the Order in 1934. (See D. Blake McDougall, John E. McDonough and Kenneth W. Tingley, *Lieutenant-Governors of the Northwest Territories and Alberta 1876-1991,* Edmonton: Alberta Legislature Library, 1991, 49.) However, I have found no listing of Walsh's name with others who became members of this Order in 1934. The Lieutenant-Governor of Ontario, for example, is mentioned as having been admitted to the Order. (See *Canadian Annual Review of Public Affairs 1934,* 100 & 535. Also see, *Edmonton Bulletin,* Thursday, 12 July 1934, 6 & *Edmonton Journal,* 13 November 1934, 12..)

79. *Edmonton Journal,* 13 July 1934.

80. *Edmonton Journal,* Monday 19 September 1949, 24.

81. *Edmonton Journal,* Tuesday, 24 November 1953, 15.

82. His Honour Percy Page to the Under Secretary of State, 13 October 1964, *Provincial Archives of Alberta,* Lieutenant-Governors private Correspondence 1960-1965, GS 84.464 A-1, J. Percy Page; *Edmonton Journal,* Monday 2 November 1964, 14 (photo).

83. *Edmonton Journal,* Saturday 19 )ctOber 1985, A8.

84. University of Alberta, *Calendar 2000/2001,* 735-737.

85. Province of Alberta, *Statutes, 1906,* Chapter 42, 382.

86. *Edmonton Journal,* 6 September 1974, 61.

87. Province of Alberta, *Statutes, 1976,* Chapter 88, 588.

88. There is a file containing several documents relating to this matter in the Provincial Archives of Alberta. See Office of Lieutenant-Governor, General Correspondence, *Provincial Archives of Alberta,* University Visitor GS 79.338 Box #3.

89. *Saint John's Edmonton Report,* 13 December 1976, 26.

90. *Saint John's Edmonton Report,* 24 January 1977, 34.

91. *Saint John's Edmonton Report,* 28 February 1977, 32.

92. University of Alberta, *Order for the Installation of the Chancellor.*

92

# III

# POWERS OF THE CROWN

The powers of the Monarch and her representatives fall into two general categories: *statutory powers* — those established by legislation; and *prerogative powers* — the authority vested in the Crown through custom, tradition and precedent. This "Royal Prerogative" includes, for example, the right to summon and dissolve the Legislature and to preside over its Opening, and the granting of honours. The most significant of the Royal Prerogative is found in continuity of government and reserve or emergency powers.

Continuity of Government

The Lieutenant-Governor has the prime responsibility of ensuring that there is always a First Minister. A general election must take place within five years after the return of the writs from the last general election. Following the election, the Lieutenant-Governor calls upon the leader of the party holding the majority of the seats in the Legislative Assembly to become the First Minister and to form a government. If no party holds a clear majority of the seats, the Queen's representative must call upon an elected member who can command a majority in the Legislature. In the history of the province of Alberta, there has never been a party in a minority position in the Legislative Assembly. Thus, for most of the province's history, the choice of the Lieutenant-Governor has generally been straightforward. Initially, the Lieutenant-Governor exercised more power in the choice of Premier than today and there have been several occasions when the Lieutenant-Governor refused to accept the resignation of a Premier until he was convinced an individual had emerged who had the support of the majority in the Legislative Assembly.

The day following his installation as Lieutenant-Governor on 1 September 1905, His Honour George Bulyea traversed the North Saskatchewan River by ferry to Strathcona and asked the newly selected leader of the Liberal party of Alberta, Alexander Cameron Rutherford, to form a government. Rutherford accepted and was immediately sworn in as Premier.[1] Although the first election in the newly constituted province had not yet occurred, Lieutenant-Governor Bulyea's choice of Premier was not surprising. The Governor General had appointed Bulyea as Lieutenant-Governor on the advice of the Canadian Prime Minister, Sir Wilfrid Laurier, who in turn was advised by the Edmonton Liberal patronage czar, Frank Oliver. Bulyea was then expected to appoint a fellow Liberal as Premier of the province.[2]

In the early years of the province, the Lieutenant-Governor meddled in the politics of Alberta more than would be acceptable today. In order to keep the Liberals in power in the midst of the Alberta and Great Waterways Railway scandal which raised unfounded charges of corruption against Premier Rutherford,[3] the Lieutenant-Governor helped to engineer the dismissal of Rutherford and his replacement by the Chief Justice of Alberta, Arthur Sifton. Upon securing Rutherford's resignation, His Honour George Bulyea wrote Sir Wilfrid Laurier, explaining that "'I am afraid that I had to do a few things that a Lieutenant-Governor is not supposed to do...but I think it was justified by the results.'"[4] With no preparation of public opinion before acting, on 26 May 1910, the Lieutenant-Governor, "in a tweed suit and a bowler hat"[5], attire which scandalized the Edmonton *Journal,* entered the Legislative Assembly and announced that he had accepted the resignation of Premier Rutherford that very morning. His Honour had manipulated the selection process to make certain that a rival of Rutherford's, William Cushing from Calgary, did not secure the Premier's job.[6]

Ensuring the province possessed a Premier became more routine after Sifton's appointment and less dependent on the Lieutenant-Governor's personal preference. Nevertheless, there were several glitches in the procedure throughout Alberta's history. With the change of government from the Liberals under Charles Stewart in 1921 to the United Farmers of Alberta (UFA), the transition of government took time. The UFA had won the election but without a designated leader who would assume the responsibility of advising the Lieutenant-Governor. Consequently, the first order of business for the UFA after defeating the Liberals was to meet in Calgary to select a leader. The natural choice was Henry Wise Wood, the spiritual leader of the movement, but when he refused, the farmers chose one of their own, Herbert Greenfield, over the lawyer, John Brownlee. By 1925, however, Greenfield had lost control of his caucus and after the closing of the Session of the Legislature, the United Farmers of Alberta party decided that John Brownlee should replace Greenfield as leader and Premier. Greenfield visited the newly appointed Lieutenant Governor, Dr. William Egbert at Government House on 23 November 1925, and tendered his resignation. He informed the Lieutenant-Governor about the wishes of the caucus and advised him to call on John Brownlee to form a government. His Honour followed his outgoing Premier's advice. Brownlee accepted the invitation and the swearing-in ceremony of the new Premier and his ministers took place in the Lieutenant Governor's office at the Legislature.[7]

When Premier Brownlee became caught up in a nasty civil action in late June 1934 as a defendant in the alleged seduction of a young woman, Vivian MacMillan, his political career came to an abrupt end amid rumours and gossip fired by Alberta newspaper titillation.[8] Immediately following the trial on the evening of 30 June, Brownlee visited the Lieutenant-Governor at Government House to inform him that he intended to resign, but would await until a successor was chosen.[9] An Edmonton caucus meeting was called after the Dominion Day holiday and settled on Gavin Reid as Brownlee's successor. Satisfied with the decision, Brownlee officially tendered his resignation to Lieutenant-Governor Walsh at noon on Thursday, 5 July. He advised His Honour that Reid was the choice of the majority of the Assembly. However, the Lieutenant-Governor refused Brownlee's resignation at that time. When Reid arrived at Government House, the Lieutenant-Governor refused to swear him in as Premier until he was ready to present His Honour with a complete cabinet.[10] After a few more days all was in order and on 10 July 1934, Gavin Reid and his new ministers entered the Lieutenant-Governor's office in late afternoon for the swearing-in ceremony; shortly thereafter, the oath was taken and the register of council signed.[11] The Lieutenant-Governor had fulfilled his duties by ensuring the province had a Premier and government. Reid would remain in office until William Aberhart and his Social Credit followers defeated the United Farmers of Alberta in the general election of August 1935.

When the Social Credit Party won the election of 22 August, William Aberhart, although leader, had not sought a seat in the Legislative Assembly at the time of the election. Thus, the Lieutenant-Governor had to be assured that Aberhart was the choice of his party for Premier. When satisfied about the party's wishes, His Honour William Walsh swore Aberhart and his government into office. Because of a pre-arranged resignation by a newly elected Social Credit member, Aberhart was able to run in a by-election. Since he was duly elected, he could remain as Premier without question.

When Ernest Manning succeeded William Aberhart who died in office on 23 May 1943, the public focused on the Lieutenant-Governor's role once again. After the spring Session of the Legislature, Aberhart had gone to Vancouver to study French and visit his daughter. While he was out of the province, Ernest Manning acted as Premier, but that was a customary arrangement of convenience and not intended as a formal sign of succession. Thus, Lieutenant-Governor Bowen turned to Manning to submit a name as Premier to him immediately after Aberhart's funeral. The Social Credit Assembly caucus met and chose Ernest Manning over Solon Low as leader.[12] Manning informed the Lieutenant-Governor of this decision and His Honour swore him in as Premier on 31 May 1943.[13]

Since the death of Aberhart in office, the transition from one Premier to another has been more routine; either elections have determined the choice of Premier or political conventions have chosen a new leader for the party in power before a Premier resigned. As in the past, in modern-day Alberta, the Lieutenant-Governor follows precedent and always makes certain an individual commands a majority in the Legislative Assembly before inviting the individual to a rather informal meeting in the Lieutenant-Governor's office in the Legislature Building and asking the politician to form a government.[14] The Lieutenant-Governor always makes certain there is a Premier to advise him on matters of state. Since the Premier is the choice of the Assembly and not the personal choice of the Lieutenant-Governor, sometimes the relationship between the Lieutenant-Governor and Premier is not always as warm as the public image suggests.

(Provincial Archives of Alberta, PG.242/1)

### Swearing-in of Lougheed Government
His Honour Grant MacEwan presides over the swearing-in of Premier Peter Lougheed's government
Friday, 10 September 1971

The Lieutenant-Governor's Relationship with the Premier

Under our responsible government system, the Lieutenant-Governor must accept the advice of the Premier who is the individual who commands the majority in the Assembly. The Crown holds all power but exercises none; the Premier holds no power but exercises all power. If the Crown refuses to accept advice from a Premier, the Crown must ask another individual to become Premier because the Crown can never act alone without someone responsible for the Crown's actions. On the other hand, the Premier can not act without the agreement of the Lieutenant-Governor. This necessity prevents a Premier from displaying too much arrogance. By having the portrait of the Monarch look down from behind the Premier in the Alberta Legislative Assembly Chamber, a Premier realizes that power is located in the Crown. This pre-eminent position of the Lieutenant-Governor within the province was remarked upon by His Honour Ralph Steinhauer. Once, when a prominent politician squeezed ahead of him in a line-up, he nonchalantly commented: "'Go ahead, I don't have to fight for my position.'"[15] On the other hand, the Lieutenant-Governor must always be aware that his Office "is no place for self-aggrandizement or private hobby horses"[16] because, by tradition and custom, he must gain the Premier's consent for his every action.

During the period the Social Credit government of Aberhart served under His Honour William Walsh, if the Lieutenant-Governor wished to discuss legal aspects of any piece of legislation, he would send for the Attorney General and his legislative counsel. The three individuals would freely discuss the measures over tea. His Honour only saw the Premier or Ministers when issues concerning various bills requiring royal assent raised questions he wished answered[17]. After The Honourable John Bowen replaced Lieutenant-Governor Philip Primrose, the relationship between the Sovereign's representative and the ministry soured.

The association between His Honour John Bowen and Premier Aberhart was limited and marked with difficulty. During the royal visit of King George VI and Queen Elizabeth in 1939, Aberhart and the Lieutenant-Governor squabbled over their respective roles while their Royal Highnesses visited Edmonton. Aberhart wanted the Lieutenant-Governor out of sight most of the time because, he maintained, "the vice-regal function was to represent the Sovereign in His Majesty's absence, not in his presence."[18] Bowen disagreed. This spat led to a certain degree of visible prickliness between the two men throughout the royal visit. Mackenzie King, the Canadian Prime Minister later claimed he spent most of his time keeping the royal couple ignorant of the petty quarrels between the Lieutenant-Governor and Premier.[19]

The personal enmity between Bowen and Aberhart had been exacerbated by Aberhart's failure to enact "Social Credit" legislation at the outset of his administration. At one point, several caucus members circulated a petition to His Honour requesting Aberhart's replacement.[20] The friction then worsened when Aberhart attempted to quell rebellion within Social Credit ranks by proposing legislation designed to keep the legislative caucus loyal to him. For example, in a brief session which opened 3 August 1937 and ended three days later, the Aberhart government brought in supposedly "Social Credit" legislation, two bills concerning banks and one dealing with civil rights which prevented an appeal to the courts questioning the validity of provincial legislation. Although these bills snuffed out the back-bench revolt for Aberhart, they raised important constitutional issues which the Lieutenant-Governor queried. Before signing these bills, the Lieutenant-Governor requested that the Premier and the Attorney General, John Hugill, come to his office for consultation. Speculation arose whether the Lieutenant-Governor would employ his very seldom used prerogative powers and reserve these bills for the pleasure of the Governor General.

When His Honour asked the Attorney General his opinion of the bills, Aberhart expected Hugill to assure the Lieutenant-Governor of his approval of them. Instead, he confided to His Honour that they were unconstitutional. Without allowing Hugill to advise the Lieutenant-Governor to withhold his assent, Aberhart broke into the conversation and insisted that His Honour sign the bills. With the Premier taking the responsibility for this action, Bowen signed[21] and the questionable bills became law until they were eventually disallowed by the Governor General. When Aberhart refused to allow His Honour to publish the proclamation of disallowance in the *Alberta Gazette*, the federal government had them published in the *Canada Gazette*.[22] These bills in a revised version were later reintroduced at a subsequent session of the Alberta Legislature, but on this occasion, the Lieutenant-Governor reserved them for the pleasure of the federal authorities[23] under statutory powers which continue to exist in the *Constitution Acts, 1867 to 1982*, ( section 55 of *The British North America Act, 1867)*. Although constitutional, Bowen's actions led to his physical removal from Government House and the closure of the Vice-regal residence by Aberhart!

In a much less dramatic fashion, another Lieutenant-Governor, His Honour Frank Lynch-Staunton, found that Premier Peter Lougheed was very much in control of the levers of power in Alberta. When the Premier wanted something done, he demanded action immediately. On one occasion when His Honour was at a dinner at the Mayfair Golf Club in Edmonton, he received word that the Premier wanted some bills signed that very night. The Premier had sent a driver to fetch the Lieutenant-Governor. On reading the bills, His Honour could see no reason for the hurry, but the Premier got his way.[24]

On another occasion, The Honourable Frank Lynch-Staunton was at Banff to open and speak at a convention. The Premier wanted to adjourn the session of the Legislature the very night His Honour was supposed to deliver his address. The Premier asked Lynch-Staunton to return to Edmonton immediately as only the Lieutenant-Governor can perform this constitutional responsibility. As was his right, the Lieutenant-Governor pulled his weight, finished his part at the convention, gave his excuses to the brass and left. After an uneventful flight back to Edmonton, His Honour was driven from the airport to the Legislature where he adjourned the session just before midnight.[25] His unenthusiastic return to the capital reminded the Premier that there was no good reason the Legislature could not be prorogued the following day except for the impatience of government members to end opposition questioning. The mere presence of the Lieutenant-Governor within the parliamentary system makes the Premier realize that he cannot dictate at will and that someone else's presence within civil society reminds him to keep the public's interest at heart.

Annoyed at His Honour Gordon Towers for musing about a spring election in 1993, Premier Klein snubbed His Honour by not visiting him to ask for a dissolution, but sent the Deputy Premier and a staff member to make the necessary arrangements. Some authorities said they were "astounded" by the Premier's actions and called them "highly unusual" and "a snub." Deputy Premier Ken Kowalski and Peter Elzinga delivered the writ to His Honour at 10:20 AM one Tuesday while Premier Klein was in Calgary preparing for a noon-hour candidate's rally and election announcement.[26] Nevertheless, the Premier got his way and His Honour signed the necessary documents to dissolve the Legislature and permit the issuing of writs for the general election. Personal pique cannot get in the way of constitutional responsibility. But obligations in matters constitutional are a two-way street: the Lieutenant-Governor has the right to be consulted by the Premier, to encourage and to warn the Premier of any untoward action which could adversely affect civil society.

The Right to be Consulted, to Encourage and Occasionally to Warn

The right to be consulted, to encourage and occasionally to warn are active prerogative powers which the Queen delegates to her Lieutenant-Governors at the provincial level in Canada. These powers, combined with the Crown's independence and respect, enable the Vice-regal representatives to act as referees and to see that the "rules of the game" are observed by those elected to govern. The meetings between the Lieutenant-Governor and the Premier are supposed to be *in camera*, outside of the public view. Behind closed doors, the Lieutenant-Governor can advise, warn and encourage a Premier. The Lieutenant-Governor is the one person with whom the Premier can be frank and from whom he should be able to ask and get sympathetic advice and encouragement. Peter Lougheed recognized this atmosphere of trust which can develop between the Premier and Lieutenant-Governor and said that Grant MacEwan "was a great mentor and counsellor to me as premier."[27] On the other hand, the Premier might lack confidence in the Vice-regal representative in the province. Because of the personality of His Honour Gordon Towers and the cool relationship between him and the Klein government, conversations which should have remained private, became public knowledge. One such occasion occurred in the spring of 1993 when the Deptuy Premier, Ken Kowalski, visited His Honour to tell him that there would be no Speech from the Throne. Rather than start a new Session of the Legislature, the government decided to continue the existing one in order that the Premier would be front-and-centre with a "state-of-the-province address".[28] Following his meeting with the Deputy Premier, His Honour told the press that the government would continue in Session for a short period and then call an election! In attempting to explain why he was not reading a Speech from the Throne, His Honour had given away a government secret—the timing of the next election. The Deputy Premier was furious and publicly complained that he was unaware "of any representatives of the Queen ever making an announcement of this nature...."[29]

    This unprecedented departure from tradition by the Lieutenant-Governor would not be the last time the uneasy relationship between His Honour and

Premier Klein would be revealed to an astonished public. His Honour Gordon Towers attempted to keep the relationship cordial and often invited the Premier into his office for a "nip" and chat. Towers enjoyed having a glass of scotch and telling political stories.[30] For his part, Premier Klein whimsically reminisced at the time of the retirement of the Honourable Gordon Towers about the ceremonial task of delivering the throne speech to His Honour at home where Towers would keep him "for at least one glass of scotch."[31] Although these encounters between the Lieutenant-Governor and his Premier are to be strictly confidential, the openness of discussions depends upon the personal relationship these two individuals engender.

(Larry Wong, *The Edmonton Journal*)

*Premier meets with Lieutenant-Governors*
Premier Ralph Klein met with the incoming Lieutenant-Governor, Bud Olson, and the outgoing Lieutenant-Governor Gordon Towers 13 April 1996

Shortly after he was installed as Lieutenant-Governor, The Honourable Ralph Steinhauer appeared to veer from constitutional practice. He made a number of statements on native affairs at the University of Calgary in a speech in the fall of 1974 and stated that he declined to rule out the possibility of refusing to sign legislation concerning native affairs with which he disagreed. Three years later in the Legislature, Grant Notley attacked Premier Lougheed who, he claimed, had asked Ottawa to muzzle His Honour for making sensitive statements on a number of issues, particularly Indian affairs. On this occasion, Notley was referring to a controversial amendment to the Land Titles Act which would restrict the filing of caveats on provincial land. Caveats had been used by First Nations people to protect native land claims. The Premier quite rightly refused to reply to this charge in this "highly confidential and delicate matter."[32] All discussions concerning the Premier and the Lieutenant-Governor were quite rightly kept confidential by the Premier.

The atmosphere of trust between the Lieutenant-Governor and her Premier was almost shattered by the Honourable Lois Hole shortly after her installation as the Queen's Vice-regal representative in Alberta. A somewhat dramatic incident erupted on the Ides of March, 15 March 2000, the anniversary of the assassination of Julius Caesar by Brutus in the Roman Senate. Her Honour Lois Hole stepped into the centre of political controversy over the infamous "Bill 11", the government proposal with respect to health care. For opponents of this legislation, the bill would enable the establishment of a two tier health system in Alberta. At a meeting in Red Deer, Her Honour casually stated that she wanted to chat with Premier Klein before giving final assent to this piece of legislation.  When the press, rightly or wrongly, suggested this remark indicated a difference of opinion between the Lieutenant-Governor and her Premier, Her Honour explained that while she was not supposed to take a political stance, she made her remarks because "Bill 11" was on everyone's mind.  She explained that "I'm hearing things and I will tell him (Klein) what I'm hearing, and I hope it will help him."[33]  Ironically, at the time of her installation, Her Honour had stated that she would not "hesitate to offer Premier Ralph Klein advice if she thinks the government is headed in the wrong direction, although she'll be careful about making public statements."[34]

This innocent comment soon became blown out of all proportion with some mischievous individuals in the press suggesting the Lieutenant-Governor was going to refuse assent if "Bill 11" passed through the Legislative process. The Leader of Her Majesty's Official Opposition called Her Honour's remarks "highly unusual" because although the Lieutenant-Governor has the right to warn and advise the Premier, she must do so in private and out of the glare of public scrutiny.  According to the constitutional expert, Allan Tupper, the Lieutenant-Governor does have the legal right under the constitution to refuse assent even if the Premier advises her to sign, yet this aspect of the constitution had become inoperative in modern times, especially when the Premier is supported by a majority in the Assembly.[35]  It came as no surprise that Her Honour clarified her position in a terse press release, issued without comment: Her Honour confirmed that she would not use her authority and decline Royal Assent to the controversial private health care bill before the Legislature.  She explained: *"For the record, I will fulfill the duty of my office recognizing the role of elected representatives in the democratic process if and when Royal Assent is sought...I have confirmed this to Premier Klein."*[36] This incident showed Her Honour that a representative of the Crown must weigh every remark, however innocuous, very carefully for its political consequences before being uttered and that the power of a Lieutenant-Governor to encourage and warn a Premier is best executed in private. Nevertheless, three years later, Her Honour again came perilously close to the line separating pageantry from politics.

On Friday evening, 6 June 2003, Her Honour Lois Hole attended the Edmonton Symphony Orchestra's commemoration of the 50th anniversary of the Coronation of Her Majesty Queen Elizabeth II for the purpose of presenting the members of the orchestra with Queen's Jubilee medals. Addressing the orchestra and audience from a podium on stage, Her Honour praised public education, public libraries and the need for the arts and criticized those who placed them in jeopardy. Newspaper accounts reported that, although Her Honour named no names, "the audience recognized the target of her admonitions as the philistines who run the provincial government."[37] Paula Simons, a columnist for the *Edmonton Journal*, reminded her readers and Her Honour that a Lieutenant-Governor is not supposed to criticize the policies of Her Majesty's government but is supposed to remain apolitical. She noted that the Honourable Lois Hole's speech at the Winspear Centre "gave a gentle but decided push to the edge of that envelope."[38] Explaining her remarks later, Her Honour said that she now had "a clearer sense of what's important"[39] because of the death of her husband, Ted, just a few months previously, and her own fight with cancer. She explained that her comments were merely "a call to all Albertans to support education."[40] Despite this explanation, some observers questioned whether Her Honour had "ventured beyond what we customarily expect lieutenant-governors to be involved in."[41] Undoubtedly, because of her popularity amongst the Albertan population, the Premier and the Minister of Learning's spokesman could only agree with Her Honour "on the importance of public education."[42] The Honourable Lois Hole appears to have great self-knowledge in assessing how close she can approach the political realm.

On 1 September 2004 at the centennial kickoff in front of the Legislature, Her Honour called on her government "to celebrate Alberta's centennial by helping the poor, spending more on art, schools and libraries and sharing some provincial wealth with poorer provinces."[43] As in the past, Her Honour was wading into public policy issues, even though earlier in the year, "she said she was striving to be non-political."[44] Premier Ralph Klein left the ceremony without commenting on the Lieutenant-Governor's comments, although the following day he said he did not mind Her Honour stating "what she would like to see done with Alberta's mounting oil and gas fortunes...." because, he claimed, he did not think she was speaking out on policy because his government had not yet developed policy.[45] Yet again, Her Honour Lois Hole demonstrated an uncanny ability to go "to the line" but not step over it into partisan politics. This instinct is valuable because the Lieutenant-Governor must give each bill Royal Assent before it becomes law.

Royal Assent

Royal Assent transforms bills into Acts of the Alberta Legislature. Given in the Queen's name by the Lieutenant-Governor, Royal Assent is the final, formal step in the legislative process. This is why bills always contain the introductory phrase: " Her Majesty, by and with the advice and consent of the Legislative Assembly of Alberta, enacts as follows."

In Canada, Royal Assent is often given in the Legislative Assembly provincially or the Senate at the federal level. In the Legislature of Alberta, the Lieutenant-Governor is informed by the Premier's Office when there are bills to receive Royal Assent. The request to give assent may occur during a Legislative Session, but most certainly at the end of each Session. The Lieutenant-Governor arrives in the Legislative Chamber, escorted by the Black Rod, and sits on the Throne. The Clerk Assistant reads all the Bills at once, giving the number of the Bill and its title. He then prays Royal Assent. The Lieutenant-Governor nods assent, but has "the right to withhold Royal Assent to any Bill, with just cause, of course, at this time."[46] In the past when a Lieutenant-Governor was always male, he wore a hat when giving royal assent. "The hat certainly makes the lieutenant-governor different from all others present in the House and thus enables him to approve of the work of his officers by tipping his hat."[47] That gesture signified approval of the legislation passed by the Legislature.

Britain abandoned this practice of giving assent in the Legislature in 1854, but King George VI, as King of Canada, assented to several bills in the Canadian Senate during his visit in 1939.[48] In describing the procedure, Bora

Laskin, who as deputy Governor General often stood in for the sovereign's representative at this ceremony explained: "I have now had practical experience of how responsible government works; I simply had to nod".[49]

After the Lieutenant-Governor gives Royal Assent to the bills before him and prorogues the Session of the Legislature, the Crown's representative then leaves as all present stand in response to the Black Rod's request: "All rise please!". Once these formalities have concluded, the press gallery then showers the floor of the Assembly with paper, a tradition of sending back to the

(Provincial Archives of Alberta, J.340)

**End of Session Press Gallery Shenanigans**
Once the Lieutenant-Governor leaves the Legislative Assembly after proroguing it, the press gallery showers the floor of the Assembly with paper, throwing back to the Members below the words they have spoken during the Session

Members the words they have sent up to the scribes in the gallery over the course of the Session. As the *Edmonton Journal* so tactfully put this procedure in 1913, "The Lieutenant-Governor and his suite retire. The House breaks up and the legislators, like school boys released from arduous tasks, respond to the pelting of papers they get from the members of the press gallery."[50]

According to our responsible government tradition, the Lieutenant-Governor must give Royal Assent to all bills if requested to do so by the Premier. However, there have been cases where the Alberta representative of the Sovereign refused Royal Assent and reserved provincial legislation for the Governor General's pleasure. Such was the case in 1937 when His Honour John Bowen refused Royal Assent to three Social Credit bills and asked the federal Justice Minister for guidance because he believed the legislation was unconstitutional. He only took this unprecedented action of reserving two bills dealing with banks and one with press censorship after Aberhart refused to submit them to the Supreme Court to determine their legality.[51] During this period of battle with the Premier, Bowen thought of dismissing Aberhart from office and forming a new ministry, a thought Mackenzie King described as "'a mad course.'"[52] Despite the fact that all three reserved bills were declared unconstitutional by the Supreme Court of Canada, and the Judicial Committee of the Privy Council refused to hear an appeal by the province of Alberta of the Supreme Court's decision,[53] this action by the Lieutenant-Governor was the affront to Premier Aberhart's advice which landed the Vice-regal representative in the street looking for suitable accommodation!

Again in June 1938 when the Provincial Treasurer, Solon Low, asked His

Honour to approve unlimited funds to establish Treasury Branches throughout the province, Bowen refused and allowed only $200,000 for the purpose. This incident represented just another deliberate wound which Aberhart believed the Lieutenant-Governor had inflicted upon his government.[54]

The Honourable Ralph Steinhauer also faced the serious question of whether to grant Royal Assent to legislation proposed by the government of the day. Native groups pressured him to delay a bill dealing with disputed land in the Fort McMurray area. His Honour met with Premier Lougheed, a land claims official and others in order to help him arrive at a responsible decision. In the end, he signed the bill because he concluded that it was within the power of the provincial legislature to decide the matter.[55] In addition to Royal Assent, the Lieutenant-Governor must give approval to money bills prior to their introduction into the Legislature while it is sitting.[56]

Appropriations for Public Spending

In Alberta, appropriations for public spending are prefaced by a request to the Lieutenant Governor from the Legislature through a resolution that certain sums "be granted to Her Majesty"—an ancient practice reflecting the hard-won control by Parliament over public funds. When passed, the appropriation is entitled "An Act for granting to Her Majesty certain sums of money for the Public Service" and includes the phrase, "The application of all Moneys expended under this Act shall be accounted for to Her Majesty." In effect, there can be no tax on the people without the permission of the Lieutenant-Governor.[57] This permission is given in the Lieutenant-Governor's office in the Legislature Building.

Proclamations and Orders-in-Council

Another duty the Lieutenant-Governor performs is the issuing of Proclamations and Orders-in-Council. Proclamations bring all, or parts of Acts into effect. Orders-in-Council are numerous and generally signed weekly. On

(Provincial Archives of Alberta, PA.4390)

*Proclamation of the Flag of Alberta*
Lieutenant-Governor Grant MacEwan proclaims the adoption of the present provincial flag of Alberta at the end of the 1st Session of the 16th Legislature
Wednesday, 1 May 1968

one occasion, The Honourable Gordon Towers blocked a substantial grant from The Honourable Ken Kowalski's department because he considered it inappropriate and flawed. Towers demanded the Order-in-Council be rewritten before he would sign.[58] Once his questions were satisfactorily answered after a five-day to and for exchange of information, the Lieutenant-Governor finally relented and signed the Order-in-Council on 1 March 1993.[59] This incident allowed Towers to claim that his actions proved that his office "is not just a rubber stamp."[60]

Crown as Custodian of Powers of the State

Truly, the Queen's representative in Alberta is essential to the exercise of all power within the provincial sphere of jurisdiction. The phrase, "humble address" to the Lieutenant-Governor, reminds us of the respect owned to the custodian of the formal powers of the State. Those who wield power on behalf of the Crown are known as "Her Majesty's Government" and the Official Opposition is known as "Her Majesty's Loyal Opposition", reflecting the allegiance of both sides of the House to a non-partisan Sovereign.

## NOTES

1. D.R. Babcock, *A Gentleman of Strathcona: Alexander Cameron Rutherford,* [Calgary]: Friends of Rutherford House and the University of Calgary Press, [1989], 27.

2. L. G. Thomas, *The Liberal Party in Alberta: A History of Politics in the Province of Alberta 1905-1921,* Toronto: University of Toronto Press, 1959, 17-18.

3. *Ibid.,* 206.

4. John T. Saywell, "The Lieutenant-Governors" in *The Provincial Political Systems, comparative essays,* eds. David J. Bellamy, Jon H. Pammett, and Donald C. Rowat, Toronto: Methuen, [1976], 302-303.

5. *Ibid.,* 89.

6. *Ibid.,* 89-94.

7. *Edmonton Journal* 23 November 1925.

8. Ernest Watkins, *The Golden Province: A Political History of Alberta,* Calgary: Sandstone Publishing Ltd., [1980], 80-81.

9. *Edmonton Journal* 3 July 1934.

10. *Edmonton Journal* 5 July 1934.

11. *Edmonton Journal* 10 July 1934.

12. Alfred J. Hooke, *30 + 5 I Know, I was there,* [Edmonton]: [Institute of Applied Art], [1971], 169.

13. Watkins, *The Golden Province,* 141-143.

14. *Edmonton Journal,* 12 July 1974, 39.

15. *Alberta Magazine,* July/August 1980, 34.

16. *The National Post,* 10 December 2001, A4.

17. David R. Elliott and Iris Miller, *Bible Bill: A Biography of William Aberhart,* [Edmonton]: Reidmore Books, [1987], 268.

18. L.P.V. Johnson and Ola MacNutt, *Aberhart of Alberta,* [Edmonton]: [Institute of Appl;ied Art], [1070], 181.

19. Elliott and Miller, *Bible Bill,* 284.

20. Norman Ward, "Hon. James Gardiner and the Liberal Party of Alberta, 1935-40", *Canadian Historical Review*, 51.3 (September 1975), 305-306.

21. Elliott and Miller, *Bible Bill*, 268.

22. Saywell, "The Lieutenant-Governors", 305.

23. *Ibid.*, 307.

24. Frank Lynch-Staunton, *Greener Pastures: The Memoires of F. Lynch-Staunton,* Edmonton: Jasper Printing Group, 1987, 41.

25. *Ibid.*, 41-42.

26. *Edmonton Journal,* 19 May 1993.

27. *Edmonton Journal,* 17 June 2000.

28. *Edmonton Sun*, 8 April 1993.

29. *Ibid.*

30. *Edmonton Journal,* 10 June 1999, A5.

31. *Edmonton Sun,* 1 April 1997, 18.

32. *Edmonton Journal,* Wednesday, 27 April 1977, 125.

33. *Edmonton Journal,* 17 March 2000, A18.

34. *Edmonton Journal,* 10 February 2000, A7.

35. *Edmonton Journal,* 17 March 2000, A18.

36. *Canadian Monarchist News/Les Nouvelles Monarchiques du Canada,* 5.2 (Spring/Summer 2000), 8.

37. *Edmonton Journal,* Sunday, 8 June 2003, B9.

38. Paula Simons, "Lois Hole pleads for public education", *Edmonton Journal,* Tuesday, 10 June 2003, A1.

39. Paula Simons, "Lois Hole pleads for public education", *Edmonton Journal,* Tuesday, 10 June 2003, A12.

40. *Edmonton Journal,* Wednesday, 11 June 2003, B1.

41. *Edmonton Journal,* Wednesday, 11 June 2003, B7.

42. *Edmonton Journal,* Wednesday, 11 June 2003, B7.

43. *Edmonton Journal,* Thursday, 2 September 2004, A1.

44. Ibid.

45. *Edmonton Journal,* Friday, 3 September 2004, A6.

46. His Honour Ralph Steinhauer to His Honour Gorden L. Bennett, Lieutenant-Governor of Prince Edward Island, 13 June 1977, *Provincial Archives of Alberta,* Correspondence with Lieutenant-Governors, L-2 "Lieutenant-Governors Other Provinces", GS 79.338 Box 9.

47. *Edmonton Journal,* 12 July 1974, 39.

48. *Ibid.,* 124.

49. David E. Smith, *The Invisible Crown: The First Principle of Canadian Government,* Toronto: University of Toronto Press, [1995], 114.

50. Frank Dolphin, *The Alberta Legislature: A Celebration,* Edmonton: Plains Publishing Inc., 1987, 78.

51. Elliott and Miller, *Bible Bill,* 273; Hooke, *30 + 5 I Know, I was there,* 137,139,141.

52. Saywell, "The Lieutenant-Governors", 306.

53. Johnson and MacNutt, *Aberhart of Alberta,* 171-175.

54. Elliott and Miller, *Bible Bill,* 280-281.

55. Dolphin, *The Alberta Legislature,* 54.

56. *Edmonton Journal,* 1 December 1985.

57. *Edmonton Journal,* 12 July 1974, 39.

58. *Edmonton Journal,* 23 December 1994.

59. *Edmonton Journal,* 11 January 1995.

60. *Edmonton Journal,* 23 December 1994.

# IV

## STATE CEREMONIAL

The Canadian state has a talent for ceremonial which is based on deep historical roots and evokes genuine emotion. These ceremonies, focused on the Crown, often carry meaning beyond those which its surface artistry might suggest. Through time, the Crown has become an institution deeply rooted in Canadian soil and one which is distinctively our own. Consequently, our state ceremony symbolizes the centrality of the Crown in Canadian political, social and cultural life. The spectacle and pageantry of the Crown at the provincial level places the Lieutenant-Governor, the provincial representative of the Crown, at the centre of these glorious civil ceremonies.

Installation

With the appointment of each Lieutenant-Governor, a ceremony embellished with pomp and pageantry takes place to instal the Vice-royal representative in office. In recent times, the installation of the Lieutenant-Governor has reverted to an earlier practice of performing the ceremony in the Legislative Chamber. In the intervening period, the ceremony took place either at Government House or in the Lieutenant-Governor's office in the Legislature. Because the speech the Lieutenant-Governors deliver at this ceremony is written by themselves, their Honours often use the installation ceremony as an occasion to set their personal stamp on their term of office.

Some Lieutenant-Governors indicated they were going to promote various themes. For example, Her Honour Lois Hole indicated that she wanted to consecrate her term to education and public health care. Hole claimed that her goal was to promote public education because she thought "'it encourages an understanding of people from all cultures. Because it's free, everyone can go and you get the wonderful mix of people, in terms of economics and culture.'"[1] In a later radio interview, she also added the promotion of a public library system and the arts.[2] Then, during the last year of her term of office, she asked Albertans "to donate money to public libraries…calling them bastions of free thought against an onslaught of corporate media." Her Honour claimed that the real battle in the 21$^{st}$ century will be "'between those who would use ignorance to serve their own greed and those who selflessly open the doors of knowledge to anyone who cares to listen.'"[3] Indicating her seriousness "to strengthen democracy and ensure that 'reading doesn't become a hobby for the rich,'" Lois Hole and her family donated a set of Her Honour's 17 books on gardening to every library in Alberta.[4] In her speech at her installation, she said that she wanted to make the office relevant by getting out and meeting ordinary Albertans. She wanted to become "the people's lieutenant-governor" and said she can always talk gardening if all else fails.[5] This reliance on the garden as a metaphor in explaining her views has served her well. Attempting to encourage Albertans to be generous with their wealth, she explained that "'Money is like manure….Spread it around and it does a lot of good. Leave it in a big pile and it does nothing but stink.'"[6] In addition, her warm and generous "hugs" have become the indelible mark of her tenure of office. This expression of warmth is a feature of her tenure which she learned from her "demonstrative, outgoing and caring" family. She once explained that "'When

I was a young girl, my grandfather couldn't hug me enough, and my father was just the same. When he'd visit our home [after I was married], he couldn't wait to hug my kids.'"[7] Her Honour Lois Hole's irrepressible concern for what is going on around her has endeared her to Albertans. In a similar way, Grant MacEwan brought down the Office of Lieutenant-Governor to the grassroots where it belongs.[8] Other Lieutenant-Governors focused on various aspects of Alberta life.

His Honour Gordon Towers opted for the promotion of the family and environmental issues such as garbage composting during his tenure of office.[9] Others could never escape their previous fame. For example, His Honour Percy Page was always identified with coaching the Edmonton Grads female basketball team, the most famous basketball team in Canadian history. Whatever the case, most Lieutenant-Governors are identified with a particular political persuasion at the outset of their role as the Queen's representative and are generally appointed because their particular political affiliation reflects that of the Canadian Prime Minister who advises the Governor General on the appointment of Lieutenant-Governors.

George Bulyea became Alberta's first Lieutenant-Governor and was sworn in at Renfrew Park before 12,000 people with the Canadian Prime Minister, Sir Wilfrid Laurier, and the Governor General, Earl Grey, present.[10] At twelve noon, the Privy Council Clerk read the King's proclamation establishing Alberta as a province and the Honourable George Bulyea as His Majesty's representative in the province. In a clear voice, under glorious Alberta sunshine and amid the cheers of thousands, His Honour took the Oath

(Provincial archives of Alberta, B. 6695)

*Installation 1ˢᵗ September 1905*
The installation of the Honourable George Bulyea at Renfrew Park in the presence of Governor General Earl Grey and Canadian Prime Minister Sir Wilfrid Laurier.

of Allegiance, the Oath of Office and signed the register. Stationed on an historic hill on a bluff overlooking Old Fort Edmonton, the Royal North West Mounted Police guns boomed forth a Royal Salute and the ceremony ended.[11]

The installation of Dr. Robert G. Brett in 1915 took place in the more traditional surrounding of the Legislative Chamber. Chief Justice Harvey administered the oath. The occasion was a "Brilliant Social Function " with 600 on the floor and in the galleries of the Legislature. The retiring Lieutenant-Governor led a party to the Speaker's throne and behind him walked Robert Brett, the famous medical doctor from Banff who made the hot springs a fashionable spa for cures.  Neither gentleman wore the British Civil Dress Uniform.  The Warrant of Commission was read, the oaths of office administered, the Great Seal presented and the register signed.[12]  Dr. Brett was a practicing physician who promoted medical education.  An active Conservative until his appointment as Lieutenant-Governor, he moved from out-of-province to Banff in 1883 to become a Canadian Pacific Railway doctor and established a hospital, sanitarium and spa in the national park.  He took a great interest in the Red Cross and helped establish the Alberta Medical Association in 1906 and became its president.  In his younger days he had served in the military and became Honorary Colonel of the Eighty-Second Battalion of the Canadian Expeditionary Force during World War I.  This ceremonial procedure for his installation in 1915 set the precedent for those who would follow except for his successor, Dr. William Egbert, who was sworn in at his home town of Calgary by Chief Justice Harvey in 1925.[13]

Like his predecessor, Dr. Egbert was a medical doctor who moved to Calgary in 1904 to practice medicine, a primary focus of his life.  He served as president of the Alberta Provincial Medical Association in 1921 and was a member of the Calgary Board of Trade.  Unlike His Honour Robert Brett, he was an active Liberal in provincial politics but never a successful candidate.  Of United Empire Loyalist stock, His Honour William Egbert was associated with the Masonic Order, the Independent Order of Foresters and the old 103rd Rifle Regiment.  He maintained a very close association with the University of Alberta.  Each year he entertained the graduates and supported the drama and debating clubs.[14]  He loved sports, especially golf and lacrosse.[15]  His installation took place in Calgary with minimal ceremony because of the timing of the event which coincided with a federal general election.

Early in September 1925, the Liberal Prime Minister called a general election for 29 October. With considerable reason, King was worried about the results. These concerns deepened as the election date drew nearer and turned to alarm just days before voting.[16] Consequently, in order to make certain a Liberal was appointed to replace the Conservative Robert Brett who was stepping down after his second term as Lieutenant-Governor, King advised the Governor General to appoint a hard working Liberal partisan to the position. William Egbert's appointment letter was hastily prepared and flown out to Calgary with the Clerk of the Privy Council on election day. Egbert had been contacted a few hours before and agreed to assume the Vice-regal responsibilities. Consequently, as soon as the official notice of appointment arrived, Dr. Egbert was sworn into office by Chief Justice Harvey of Alberta. This appointment had been made in such haste that Egbert told reporters immediately following the installation ceremony that "'I haven't made any plans yet...and don't know how soon I will be going to Edmonton.'"[17] The announcement of Dr. William Egbert's appointment as Lieutenant-Governor was publicized in newspapers full of coverage of inconclusive election results which saw the Liberals in a minority position and the Prime Minister defeated in his own riding. Mackenzie King had advised the Governor General to make Egbert's appointment just in time because immediately following the election, Governor General Baron Byng of Vimy told King he would not make any more political appointments until Parliament had met and the House of Commons had decided who should be Prime Minister of Canada, Mackenzie King or his rival, the Conservative, Arthur Meighen.[18]

By the time the next Lieutenant-Governor was to be appointed after Egbert's term had ended, the Conservatives had a majority in the House of Commons and the Governor General, of necessity, accepted the advice of his Conservative Prime Minister, R. B. Bennett. Therefore, with a return to political stability at the federal level, the haste and simplicity of His Honour William Egbert's installation could be replaced with more thoughtfulness, pomp and ceremony in 1931 for the swearing in of a former Conservative, lawyer and Justice of the Supreme Court of Alberta, The Honourable William Walsh. After leaving Ontario and a law partnership with the infamous D'Alton McCarthy of the Equal Rights Association fame, and before settling in Alberta, Walsh had practiced law in the Yukon for four years (1900-1904). For his work in the north, Walsh was made a King's Counsel. Following in his father's footsteps, Walsh became involved in Conservative politics upon his arrival in Alberta. Although never elected to office provincially, he organized behind the scenes for the party. As a result of his ability and political connections, he was appointed to the Alberta Supreme Court trial division in 1912 and there affectionately earned the name of "Daddy" Walsh for his "firm and just" decisions on the bench. The Honourable William Walsh sentenced eighteen men and women to die for murder, the most famous case being the conviction for murder of Emilio Picarielle and Florence Lassandro for killing an Alberta Provincial Police constable in 1922 in the Crow's Nest Pass prohibition case. Florence Lassandro became the first woman hanged in Alberta as a result of this conviction.[19] William Walsh was very prominent in golf circles and kept a silver golf cup he had won in Scarborough Ontario in 1922 on his office mantle during his term of office. Other sports such as cricket, tennis, lacrosse and curling also fascinated him. Just before being appointed to the Office of Lieutenant-Governor, The Honourable William Walsh was transferred to the Appeal Court of Alberta as senior puisne judge of the Alberta Supreme Court.[20]

His Honour William Walsh became Lieutenant-Governor in warm sunshine under a brilliant sky on 5 May 1931. The swearing in occurred in the Legislative Chamber before a large and distinguished gathering including representatives from the provincial government, militia, legal profession and society in general. The spacious entrance hall and main stairway were decorated with flowering plants and ferns, and a crimson carpet stretched from the lower step to the main portico outside, through the main doors and up the marble steps to the Legislative Chamber. In mid-afternoon the new Lieutenant-Governor and Bertha Walsh drove up and were escorted to the Privy Council Chamber where the Premier and cabinet were introduced. Carrying a large bouquet of crimson roses, Bertha Walsh left for her seat near the dias in the Legislature Chamber before her husband. Shortly thereafter, the Vice-regal procession entered the Chamber. Officers of the militia, aides to the Lieutenant-Governor and his private Secretary led the way to the front of the dias. They were followed by members of the Alberta judiciary, Assistant Secretary of the Privy Council of Canada and others. The Honourable William Walsh was dressed in black morning coat and dark gray-stripped trousers. He had placed a rose in his buttonhole and carried his tall silk hat. He entered

*Installation 5th May 1931*
The installation of the Honourable William Walsh in the Legislative Assembly

(Glenbow Archives, ND3-577/a)

with the Premier, John Brownlee, who escorted him to the Throne. The actual ceremony was brief but impressive. The oath was administered by Chief Justice Harvey. There were two: an Oath of Allegiance and an Oath of Office. The Lieutenant-Governor was then presented with the Great Seal of the Province of Alberta which His Honour committed to the safe custody of the Provincial Secretary. When presented with the Great Seal, The Honourable William Walsh turned to Premier Brownlee and said: "Shall I put it in my pocket?" The

(Glenbow Archives, ND3-577/c)

*Installation 5th May 1931*
His Honour William Walsh and his wife Bertha leave the Legislature Building

new Lieutenant-Governor was congratulated by the Premier and his wife, members of the cabinet, officers present and aides. There was an informal reception at the foot of the dias and hundreds from the main floor of the Assembly shook His Honour's hands. The Lieutenant-Governor and his wife then left and drove off to Government House, their new home.[21]

As His Honour William Walsh drove from the installation ceremony, little did he know that during his term of office, the Alberta Legislature would pass a resolution asking the Governor General not to appoint any more Lieutenant-

Governors as an economy measure after Walsh's term had expired. The resolution proposed that Government House be turned into a sanitorium. Ottawa never took this motion seriously because of its flaunting of constitutional requirements.[22]

When his successor was installed, William Walsh left Edmonton before the ceremony and was given a farewell at the railway station on 1 October 1936 a few hours before the new Lieutenant-Governor was installed. He departed for Calgary en route for the Pacific coast.[23] Colonel Philip Primrose was sworn in as his successor in a Legislative Chamber where the galleries were packed. A reception was held there and then the official party returned to the Lieutenant-Governor's office before departing the building and inspecting a Royal Canadian Mounted Police guard of honour at the front entrance.[24] Unfortunately, soon after his swearing in ceremony, His Honour Philip Primrose was confined to bed. A gentleman, strict disciplinarian who erupted from time to time with whip-lash flashes of sarcasm, died after less than six months in office.[25]

The successor to Philip Primrose, John C. Bowen, made history because he became the first Lieutenant-Governor to be sworn in while the Legislature was in session.[26] This situation resulted because of Colonel Primrose's untimely death. Although leader of the official Liberal Opposition at the time of his appointment, Bowen was a gifted speaker and a good choice for the Vice-regal Office. He was a noted monarchist who had chastised the Speaker of the Legislative Assembly several times for not saying a prayer for the King at the opening of each day's sitting. Bowen was helped in his "suggestion" by a fellow supporter of the Crown, the well known and liked Edmonton military officer, William "Billy" Griesbach who brought his regiment to the gallery one day. With the Canadian military looking down upon him, the Speaker, Oran MacPherson, said a prayer for the King![27]

At a brief ceremony in the Legislative Chamber on 22 March 1937, John Bowen was installed as Lieutenant-Governor. The crowded galleries looked on as Chief Justice Harvey administered the oaths. Following this ritual, His Honour left the Chamber and returned to the Lieutenant-Governor's office in the Legislature Building in order to allow the Legislature to resume the business it had interrupted six days previously due to the death of His Honour Philip Primrose.[28]

Early in 1950, His Honour John Bowen left office because of poor health and John J. Bowlen was installed as Lieutenant-Governor on 1 February. During a simple but impressive ceremony in the Legislative Chamber, the new Lieutenant-Governor took the oaths of office before Chief Justice O'Connor of the Appellate Division of the Supreme Court of Alberta. An informal reception was then held in the Lieutenant-Governor's office.[29] His Honour John Bowlen made history by becoming the only Lieutenant-Governor to have a mountain named after him. In 1958, the name Mount Bowlen was given to "peak 3" of the Wenkchemna Range. This peak can be seen from Moraine Lake in Banff National Park and is 10,043 feet high.[30] The Honourable John Bowlen was certainly "a Vice-regal cowboy" who was one of Canada's most successful old-time ranchers, owning the largest horse herd of 3,000 at one

(City of Edmonton Archives, EA10-1478)

## Mount Bowlen
His Honour John Bowlen points out the mountain named after him in 1958

point in his career near Medicine Hat and the second largest sheep herd in the country. He also raised cattle just north of the Montana border. Very punctual, His Honour arrived at the office at 8:00 AM, finished his desk work quickly so that he was ready to meet and chat with the Monarch's subjects early in the day. His "unusual personal popularity" certainly propelled him into an extension of his appointment as Lieutenant-Governor for a second five-year term.[31] The respect he attained in office was in indirect proportion to the simplicity of his installation ceremony.

During the final years of the Ernest Manning Social Credit government, the installation ceremony of Lieutenant-Governors was circumscribed and only the essential requirements performed. The following two Lieutenant-Governors were sworn in at the Lieutenant-Governor's office in the Legislature Building. Percy Page, appointed on 19 December 1959, was a non-smoker and teetotaler. Page was a world famous basketball coach who brought a very formal approach to the office of Lieutenant-Governor.[32] Upon his arrival at the Legislature on Monday, 21 December 1959, he was conducted to the Lieutenant-Governor's third floor suite. Dressed in a dark blue business suit, Percy Page took the oaths of office. The Premier, Ernest Manning, members of his cabinet as well as Maude Page and their daughter were present.[33]

At the same location in 1966 Grant MacEwan was sworn into office on 6 January. While the Chief Justice, S. Bruce Smith, administered the oaths, His Honour's wife, Phyllis, Premier Ernest Manning, the retiring Lieutenant-Governor, Percy Page, and the provincial cabinet looked on.[34] His Honour Grant MacEwan embodied everything western Canada stood for, "the spirit of

(Provincial Archives of Alberta, PA.674/1)

*Installation 19th December 1959*
The Honourable Percy Page takes the oath of office in the
Lieutenant-Governor's 3rd floor suite in the Legislature Building

(Glenbow Archives NA-5302-2)

*Installation 6th January 1966*
The installation of Grant MacEwan in the presence of the
outgoing Lieutenant-Governor and the then
Premier Ernest Manning

the region, the sense of co-operativeness, of sharing, of volunteerism, of rugged individualism, of simply being at one with the land."[35] There were contradictions too: His Honour Grant MacEwan had been a vegetarian since 1956 and represented the Crown in a province renowned for its ranching community. An ardent environmentalist, he encouraged the preservation of nature in a province which was often careless of the stewardship of its bountiful natural resources. Like some of his noted predecessors as Lieutenant-Governor, he refused to serve liquor when he hosted functions but never refused invitations to events where alcohol was present. His humbleness, seen by his insistence on sitting in the front, rather than the back seat of his chauffeur-driven Vice-regal car, endeared him to many Albertans. Grant MacEwan's popularization of the history of the West in books he published even while Lieutenant-Governor overshadowed his various idiosyncrasies. The day of his installation was marked by the relentless, nerve-racking energy he would always put into the office of Lieutenant-Governor.[36] His Honour Grant MacEwan served as Vice-regal representative of the Queen during the transition from the Social Credit government to the Conservative Peter Lougheed administration.

While Peter Lougheed was Premier, all installations were carried out at Government House. In 1974, Chief Justice Bruce Smith presided over the installation of Ralph Steinhauer with Premier Lougheed, former Lieutenant-Governor Grant MacEwan, the cabinet and 100 invited guests present.[37] His Honour, Ralph Steinhauer, a treaty Indian from the Saddle Lake Reserve, was joined by his wife, his brothers and sisters, 5 children and 15 of his 16 grandchildren on 2 July 1974 for a simple ceremony lasting thirty minutes. The simplicity and brevity of the ceremony did not belie the importance of the event. As the Premier said: "This office is becoming more and more important year after year."[38] His Honour Ralph Steinhauer was adopted by his stepfather, joined the post office and also farmed. He began as a member of the United Farmers of Alberta, but joined the Liberals for whom he ran unsuccessfully in 1963. He founded and was President of the Indian Association of Alberta and was President of the Alberta Indian Development Corporation. He also served in many other First Nations' organizations in the province and was thus a natural choice to become the first treaty Indian to serve as Lieutenant-Governor in Canada.

Following a pattern developed for the installation of His Honour Ralph Steinhauer, Frank Lynch-Stauton was sworn in at Government House in a 30 minute ceremony with the former Lieutenant-Governor also present.[39] His Honour Frank Lynch-Staunton was a rancher who was active in Alberta public affairs. He rose to the rank of Major in the Canadian Militia before he retired in 1943. A personal friend of the family of Prime Minister Joe Clark, he was appointed by His Excellency Edward Schreyer as Lieutenant-Governor of Alberta on the advice of the Canadian Prime Minister. His Honour Frank Lynch-Staunton was followed in office by Her Honour Helen Hunley who was also sworn in at Government House in 1985. It was a short ceremony with Chief Justice Kenneth Moore administering the oaths before friends and colleagues in the reception hall of Government House.

An important piece of Alberta's material history, "a wood-and-velvet

*Installation 18<sup>th</sup> October 1979*
The installation of the Honourable Frank Lynch-Staunton at Government House

(Provincial Archives of Alberta, J.4754/1)

throne" was a feature of these ceremonies at Government House. The chair is a symbol of the monarchy and has a long and curious history. According to a former Speaker of the Legislature, Gerry Amerongen, the chair was given to Herbert Wilson when he retired as Speaker of the North West Territories Assembly in 1888. "It was an occasional custom to give the retiring Speaker his chair." The family returned the important historical object to the province in 1945 and it was placed in a corner of the Legislative Assembly where it gathered dust until 1972. Amerongen ordered it out and stored elsewhere. Kept at the Provincial Museum, the Speaker's Chair has been transformed into a Vice-regal throne and is now brought out for ceremonies involving the

### The Throne
The Honourable Bud Olson seated on the Chair at Government House used for official occasions, 30th November 1996.

Lieutenant-Governor at Government House.[40]

For Her Honour Helen Hunley, decorum often won out over impetuosity.[41] She explained that there was a "certain amount of protocol which I demand on behalf of my office...though I have more fun with events like [my annual] skating party where protocol was removed—although not totally."[42] Even family and friends were not allowed to call her by her first name when she was appearing officially as Lieutenant-Governor. She explained her demands of protocol by saying that "it's not Helen Hunley that's there, it's the lieutenant-governor and so she should be called Your Honour...."[43]

Born at Acme, Helen Hunley spent most of her childhood on a farm south of Delia where her parents grew grain and raised horses and cattle. The family of eleven children were blown out and dried out in the 1930s and were poor like most others in the area. After finishing high school at Rocky Mountain House, Helen Hunley became a telephone operator in southern Alberta before joining the Canadian Women's Army Corps in 1941. After the war she eventually bought a farming and implements dealership in Rocky Mountain House. With experience on the town council and as Mayor, she entered provincial politics in 1971 and became a minister without portfolio in Lougheed's government. After serving in two other portfolios, she resigned in 1979. Then, in 1985, this "kid in hand-me-down coats chasing gophers" from rural Alberta became the Queen's representative in the province.[44]

Her Honour Helen Hunley was the last Lieutenant-Governor to be installed at Government House. With the appointment of Gordon Towers, the province returned to the traditional method of installation at the Legislature.

(Public Archives of Alberta, 95.48/89-04847)

### Her Honour Helen Hunley
The Honourable Helen Hunley seated on the "wood-and-velvet throne" at Government House in 1989

(Steve Simon, The Edmonton Journal)

### Installation 11$^{th}$ March 1991
The installation of the Honourable Gordon Towers at the Legislature of Alberta

On 11 March, in a 45 minute ceremony in the Legislative Assembly, Gordon Towers was installed. He wore a top hat and morning coat. Chief Justice Laycroft of the Appeal Court of Alberta administered the oaths. Following the installation, His Honour inspected the 100-member guard from Canadian Forces Base Edmonton and he and his wife greeted guests in a receiving line while a military band played throughout a reception.[45] Both the outgoing Lieutenant-Governor, Helen Hunley and the incoming Vice-regal representative, Gordon Towers gave an address.[46]

His Honour Gordon Towers never pulled his punches.[47] He turned his back on fellow Albertan Joe Clark and supported Brian Mulroney in his successful Tory leadership bid in 1983. Towers always had "a special relationship" with Mulroney because their "goals were always the same."[48] Towers was a great storyteller and poet and dedicated his life at an early age to besmirch the Liberals' reputation at every opportunity.[49]

Like his predecessor, Alberta's fourteenth Lieutenant-Governor, The Honourable H. A. "Bud" Olson was installed in an impressive ceremony 17 April 1996 in the Legislative Assembly Chamber. His Honour was called by his nickname since childhood, the source of which remains a mystery. He was born into a modest Norwegian immigrant family in the tiny village of Iddesleigh surrounded by the grassland stubble of southern Alberta. After completing highschool at Medicine Hat, Olson bought the family store in 1946 and three years later began buying up land, raising cattle and planting wheat and barley crops. After entering politics as an elected Social Credit Member of Parliament in 1957, he turned his store into a museum of local history. Despite his crossing the floor to the Liberals in 1967 and his cabinet positions and call to the Senate in 1977, his roots remained on his ranch and with his family throughout his life. A straightforward, genuine and honest individual[50] who "loved gambling, gadgets and Chinese food"[51] His Honour "Bud" Olson arrived to the thunder of cannons in a 15-gun salute on the Legislature grounds to assume the highest office in the province. The installation ceremony was marked by a trumpet fanfare hailing His Honour's entrance to the Legislative Chamber and by a string ensemble playing Mozart at his exit. Eyes became misty as the outgoing Lieutenant-Governor, His Honour Gordon Towers tipped his familiar grey hat to the assembled dignitaries in the Legislative Assembly as he made his farewell exit.[52] His Honour "Bud" Olson without hesitation accepted his constitutional administrative role which suited him more than the ceremonial aspects of the position. When poor health forced his early retirement, he was succeeded by Alberta's eminent and much published gardener, Lois Hole.

In a "burst of pomp and pageantry", Lois Hole became Alberta's fifteenth Lieutenant-Governor. Her Honour was a successful businesswoman, best-selling author of gardening books, education advocate and community supporter who unknowingly prepared for the Vice-regal Office as Chancellor of the University of Alberta. Lois Hole was installed on 10 February 2000 in the Legislative Assembly Chamber. As she arrived at the Legislature Building, a 15-gun cannon salute echoed in the background. The new Vice-regal representative had to inspect the scarlet-clad Lord Strathcona's Horse (Royal Canadians) honour guard from a wheelchair after fracturing her heel two

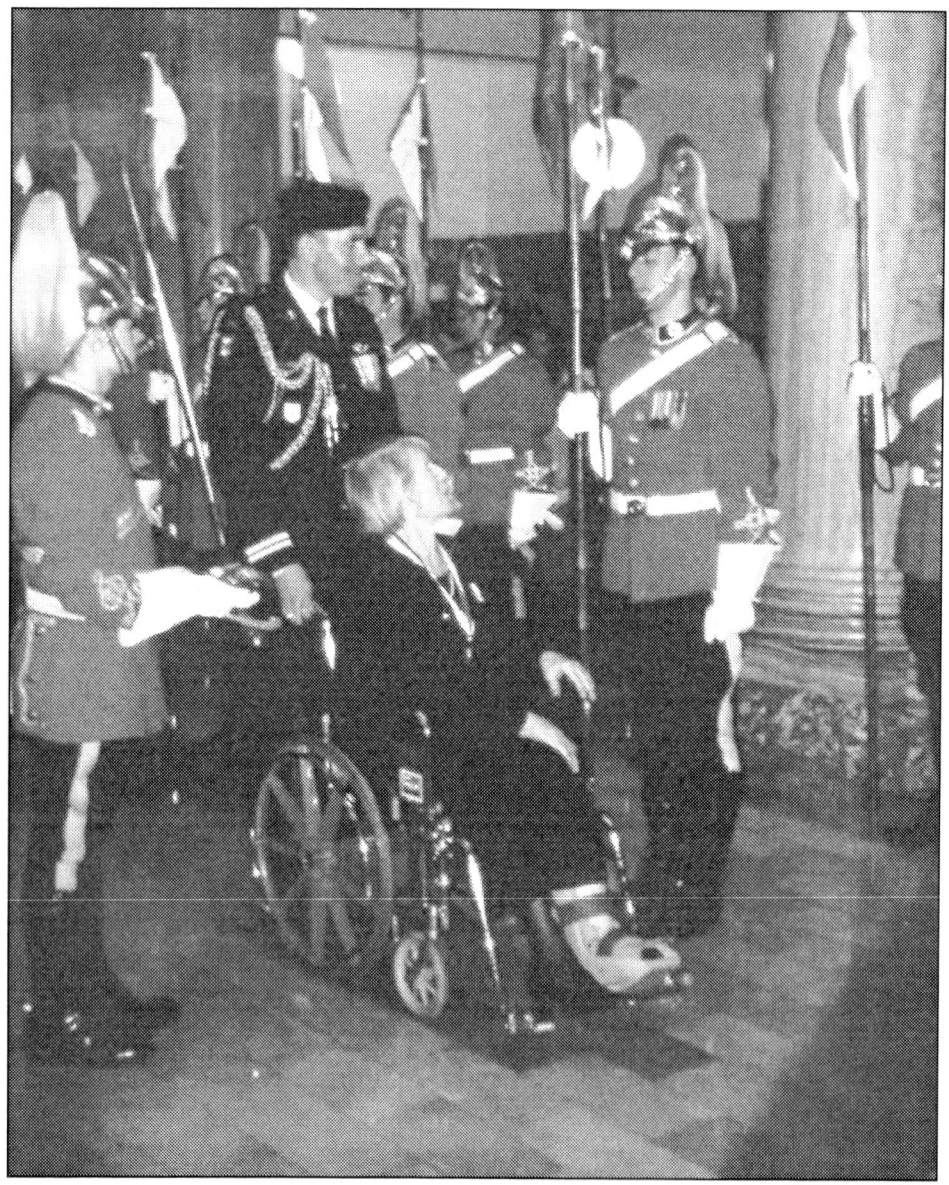

(Courtesy of LtCol Frank Kozar, Edmonton)

## Installation 10$^{th}$ February 2000
Her Honour Lois Hole inspects Lord Strathcona's Horse (Royal Canadians) at her installation in the Legislature rotunda.

weeks previously when she tripped on a podium at a banquet. When all appeared ready for the ceremony inside the Legislative Chamber to begin, the several hundred officials and guests were invited to stand. They stood and remained standing for several minutes, but the new Lieutenant-Governor did not appear! Unknown to the dignitaries and other guests, complications surfaced while Lois Hole was being wired for sound. She wore a black skirt and jacket with a single strand of white pearls, a gift from her husband Ted. Unfortunately, she did not have an inside pocket to carry sound equipment. Improvisation carried the day, but also caused a delay. It was later reported that the Gentlemen's Escort present turned away as she was "miked". How she was "miked" remains a mystery![53] Finally all was in order and Chief Justice Catherine Fraser of the Alberta Court of Appeal was able to preside over the swearing in ceremony.[54]

Overcome by emotion, Her Honour Lois Hole broke into tears at one point when she realized how wonderful this position really was. She explained that the words she was reading, their meaning, the ceremony, the music, "The moment got the better of me".[55] Premier Klein jokingly said of her expertise in gardening that one of her duties could be to make sure the ground keepers maintain all the magnificent flowers and shrubs to the highest standards. "But whether it's poinsettias or politics, or eucalyptus or universities, her pride in this country is matched only by her dedication to her new responsibilities," he added.[56]

There were sour notes as well as sobs as the Lieutenant-Governor was installed. As Lois Hole entered the Assembly Chamber, the notes from one of the Edmonton Symphony Orchestra musicians were "so off on a fanfare trumpet that even the musically disinclined jerked back their necks." Nevertheless, the proceedings continued without hesitation, but needless to say, the offending musician did not stay for the reception which followed![57] A more "note perfect" Royal Canadian Artillery Band played the music for that affair. Possibly thinking of the errant trumpeter, Neil Wilkinson, the Capital Health Authority Chair said, paying Her Honour the greatest compliment: "All other lieutenant-governors will be judged by her performance."[58] Neil Wilkinson was not only referring to Her Honour Lois Hole's dignity and bearing under the trying condition of being confined to a wheelchair at her installation, but was predicting her graceful fulfilment of the many functions she would be called upon to undertake in the future.

Opening of the Legislature

Following the installation ceremony, the most important public duty a Lieutenant-Governor is called upon to perform is to open each Session of the Provincial Legislature with the reading of the Speech from the Throne. The Legislature of Alberta comprises the Lieutenant-Governor and the elected Members of the Assembly (Alberta never possessed an Upper Chamber). The Lieutenant-Governor, representing the Queen and on behalf of the people, is responsible for bringing together the elected members for deliberation and for releasing them at the end of their deliberations. Thus the Lieutenant-Governor dissolves the Legislature to call an election and once the people have chosen their representatives, summons the Legislature again in the Queen's name.

Between elections, the Queen's representative prorogues the Sessions and recalls the members. At the Opening of each Session of the Legislative Assembly, the Lieutenant-Governor reads the *Speech from the Throne*. This document is prepared by the government of the day and outlines its policy and programmes for the upcoming Legislative Session.

In January 1642, King Charles I of Britain entered the House of Commons with an armed escort planning to arrest five Members of Parliament who were fighting most actively for the rights of Parliament against the power of the Sovereign. Having been warned of the King's intentions, they were not present when the authorities arrived to arrest them. Ever since, the Monarch has not been allowed in the House of Commons. To symbolize the independence of the House of Commons, the Monarch must read the Speech from the Throne from the Upper House. However, because the Canadian provinces are all unicameral, the Sovereign's representative delivers the speech in the Legislative Assembly Chamber.[59]

The Lieutenant-Governor arrives at the Legislature Buildings to a 15-gun salute. The Crown's representative is met by the Gentlemen Escorts, the Premier, the Speaker of the Assembly, the Senior Officer of the Armed Forces in the area, the Commander of K-Division of the Royal Canadian Mounted Police and the Lieutenant-Governor's Principal Secretary, on the steps of the building. When the weather is clement, the Lieutenant-Governor takes the Royal Salute and then inspects the Guard of Honour assembled in front of the Legislature or if weather is bad, enters the building and inspects the Guard of Honour inside the rotunda. Then the Vice-regal representative proceeds past the fountain in the centre of the rotunda—a structure installed to honour the visit to the province of Queen Elizabeth II in 1959[60]---to his offices where the Aide-de-camps, Gentlemen Escorts and their wives gather. The Aide-de-camps then conducts the spouses to their seats on the floor of the Assembly Chamber.

The Premier, the Clerk and the Gentleman Usher of the Black Rod who also serves as the Sergeant-at-Arms for the Legislative Assembly when the Crown's representative is not present, leave the Assembly Chamber to attend the Lieutenant-Governor. Alberta is the only province that has a "black rod", a sign of how very traditional the province is.[61] The Mace is draped in the Legislative Assembly and the assembled dignitaries await the Lieutenant-Governor's arrival. The original Mace which was used from 1905 until 1955 is on display by the Speaker's Office. The present Mace was a gift presented by the Provincial Civil Service Association to the Assembly to celebrate the fiftieth anniversary of Alberta's entry into Confederation as a province. The Vice-regal party arrives at the Assembly doors to find them closed, a custom which survives from the days when the House of Commons in England feared royal displeasure and barred their doors against hostile royal incursions. The Gentleman Usher of the Black Rod knocks on the Legislature Assembly main doors three times with the flat bottom of his cane. Since 1991 he "had used a plain piece of black dowelling with brass on the end."[62] In January 1998, "the Legislative Assembly of Alberta received a finely crafted new Black Rod as a gift from the Royal Canadian Legion"[63] into which was fixed a solid gold sovereign. The Parliament of Sri Lanka donated the ebony for the shaft of the rod and the Parliament of the United Kingdom donated a 1905 gold sovereign for the base.⁶⁴ The Associate Sergeant-at-Arms asks permission of the Speaker of the Legislative Assembly for the Lieutenant-Governor to enter and when permission is given, he opens the doors. Proceeded by the Gentleman Usher of the Black Rod, His Honour enters the Assembly Chamber to a fanfare followed by the Premier and the Clerk.⁶⁵ The Lieutenant-Governor walks down the central aisle, past the assembled guests to the throne.

In 1980, the people of Edmonton presented the Legislative Assembly with an arched canopy to the Speaker's Chair (used as the throne by the

(Jim Cochrane, *The Edmonton Journal*)

### Speech from the Throne
His Honour Gordon Towers with his wife Doris Towers reading the Speech from the Throne, 14 March 1991, under the arched canopy, a gift to the province from the people of Edmonton in 1980

148

Lieutenant-Governor) to commemorate the 75th anniversary of the province. The Alberta Coat of Arms displayed above the Speaker's Chair since 1911 were removed and replaced by a carving of the Alberta Coat of Arms mounted on the arch.[66] As an integral part of the canopy, the Coat of Arms of Alberta signify that the Speaker's Chair is the Throne used by the Lieutenant-Governor representing the Sovereign.

(City of Edmonton Archives, EA128-9)

*Legislative Session Opening*
The Honourable George Bulyea opening the province of Alberta's First Legislative Session at the Thistle Rink, 15 March 1906

(Glenbow Archives, NC-6-527)

### Legislature Opening 1912
His Honour George Bulyea leaving the Legislature after reading the Speech from the Throne at the opening of the Legislative Session

(Glenbow Archives, ND-3-5045d)

### 15-Gun Vice-regal Salute
Vice-regal Gun Salute at the opening of the Alberta Legislature 1929

### Honour Guard Inspection
His Honour John Bowlen inspecting the Guard of Honour before the opening of the Legislative Session in the 1950s

(City of Edmonton Archives EA10-1491)

### Alberta Legislature Opening February 2002
Her Honour Lois Hole arriving at the Legislature for the opening of the Legislative Session

(Photo Courtesy of Lt Col Frank Kozar, Edmonton)

The Lieutenant-Governor proceeds to mount the steps to the throne and as he sits down, he motions to all in the Assembly to take their seats. The male Lieutenant-Governors are dressed in morning suit and top hat while the female Lieutenant-Governors are dressed in long formal gowns. They sit with the television lights focused on them, making the Lieutenant-Governor "hotter than hell" according to His Honour Frank Lynch Staunton.[67] The Honourable Grant MacEwan was the last Lieutenant-Governor to wear the formal dark blue, military-looking British Civil Dress Uniform with the admiral's style hat with feathers. Because of the cost of the uniform which the Lieutenant-Governor himself had to bear, His Honour Ralph Steinhauer decided just to wear a morning coat with top hat. Despite his own clothing allowance, Premier Peter Lougheed refused to provide funds for the Lieutenant-Governor to buy a gold braided uniform. Once in the past, at the February Opening of the Legislature in 1952, His Honour John Bowlen opened the Legislature without the British Civil Dress Uniform and dispensed with the honour guard in deference to the death of King George VI just days before the ceremony.[68]

The Speaker announces that the Lieutenant-Governor will read the speech to open the sitting of the Legislature. The Private Secretary of His Honour, usually a female in recent years, then comes forward, curtsies, and hands over the speech which she has dutifully carried in her hands covered with white gloves. The Lieutenant-Governor then proceeds to read the document. Following the reading, the Premier and the Lieutenant-Governor walk down the aisle out of the Chamber together. As His Honour Frank Lynch-Staunton was leaving, he momentarily forgot he was wired for sound and raised much

152

**Legislature Opening**
His Honour Grant MacEwan receiving the Speech he is about to read from his private secretary.

(The Provincial Archives of Alberta, PA.5093/1)

**Legislature Opening**
His Honour Bud Olson arriving for the opening of the Alberta Legislature, 27 January 1998.

(Photo courtesy of LtCol Frank Kozar, Edmonton)

153

### Throne Speech
### 8 March 1990

Lieutenant-Governor Hunley and Premier Don Getty are escorted from the Legislature Chambers after the Throne Speech

(Joanne Tymafichuk, *The Edmonton Journal*)

(Shaughn Butts, *The Edmonton Journal*)

### Throne Speech, 10 April 2001

Her Honour Lois Hole and Premier Ralph Klein enter the Legislature for the Throne Speech

laughter as he could be distinctly heard by all assembled confide to the Premier: "that is damned hard work."[69]

At the bottom of the Grand Staircase in the Legislature Building, the Lieutenant-Governor and his wife, the Premier and his spouse and the Speaker and his wife greet. In the past, some of the receptions were held in the Legislative Library. After an appropriate period of time, the Lieutenant-Governor retires to his office in the Legislature for a smaller reception for family members, the Gentlemen Escorts and their spouses, and a few friends. He then leaves without ceremony to return to his official residence. The ceremony and pageantry connected with the *Speech from the Throne* thus comes to an end.

While occasions of spectacle filled with pomp and circumstance, the Opening and Closing of Legislative Sessions have not been without controversy. In 1910, His Honour George Bulyea was roundly criticized in the press for going to the Legislature wearing a tweed suit and a "bowler" hat in order to prorogue the Legislature.[70] When His Honour, Gordon Towers was ill with pneumonia in 1996 and could not read the speech, the task was done by the Administrator, Mister Justice John McClung, the grandson of Nellie McClung. This was the first time since 1948 a Lieutenant-Governor had not read *The Speech from the Throne*.[71] On this occasion, the Administrator became an object of derision because of his apparel. Mr. Justice McClung eschewed the traditional top hat for a less formal look and care for his broken right wrist also required an extra touch of informality. In spite of a somewhat dishevelled appearance, he managed to mumble his way through a rather truncated Speech from the Throne. After the ceremony, the mayor of Edmonton, His Worship Bill Smith, thought he liked what was in the speech, but complained that "Where I was sitting...I found it difficult to hear."[72] On another occasion, the *Edmonton Journal* criticized His Honour, "Bud" Olson for wearing a "folksy fedora" to read *The Speech from the Throne* in 1998.[73]

Today, *The speech from the Throne* ceremony is televised on local cable channels. This tradition began in a most inauspicious way. His Honour John Bowen objected when Premier Aberhart wanted the Opening broadcast on radio in February 1940 to help secure the election he was about to advise the Lieutenant-Governor to call.[74] Slowly, however, the tradition of broadcasting this supreme moment of our political life on radio, and then on television, became acceptable and allowed the Monarchy in Alberta to enter the modern age of communication.

Swearing in the Premier and MLAs

Besides reading the Speech from the Throne, there are other duties the Lieutenant-Governor performs. After each election, the Lieutenant-Governor administers the Oath of Allegiance to all Members of the Legislative Assembly in the Legislative Assembly Chamber itself. In a separate ceremony, usually at Government House, the Lieutenant-Governor administers the oath of office to cabinet ministers and hands them their commissions.[75] If a Minister changes portfolio or is elevated from the back benches to fill a cabinet post after a government has been in office for some time, this latter ceremony occurs in the Legislative office of the Lieutenant-Governor. Gordon Taylor entered into the

*Swearing in Ceremony*
(Photo courtesy of Grant Mitchell)
Her Honour Helen Hunley presides over the swearing in of Grant Mitchell as an Alberta MLA with Liberal Leader Nick Taylor looking on

Social Credit cabinet of Premier Manning in this manner in 1950.⁷⁶

In recent times, Premier Ralph Klein clashed with His Honour Gordon Towers over these procedures. Their first disagreement occurred over the logistics of the swearing in ceremony of Klein's first cabinet upon his election as leader of the Conservative party in December 1992. The Lieutenant-Governor wanted the swearing in, by tradition, at Government House while Klein wanted "a people ceremony" at the Legislature Building. As a compromise, there was a small formal ceremony at Government House to satisfy the Lieutenant-Governor, followed by a major event for 2,500 at the Legislature Building.[77] In order to demonstrate his annoyance, in April 1993, Premier Klein did not have a "Speech from the Throne" to re-open the Legislature, but rather he gave a "state of the province address" himself and continued the Session which had begun under his predecessor, Premier Don Getty.[78]

(Walter Tychnowicz, The Edmonton Sun)

*Swearing in Ceremony at Government House*
*14 December 1992*
Lieutenant-Governor Gordon Towers congratulates the Honourable Ralph Klein on the occasion of his being sworn in as Premier of Alberta

Greeting Official Visitors

Another function the Lieutenant-Governor undertakes on behalf of the people of Alberta is to greet certain official visitors to the province. The most important of these visitors are The Queen or her personal representatives such as members of the Royal Family and Governors General.

The first reigning Monarch to make an official visit to the province of Alberta was Their Majesties King George VI and Queen Elizabeth, in 1939. One of the great social events of the royal tour was a reception hosted by His Honour John Bowen. The social occasion was complicated by the political and very public quarrel between the "stiffly proper" Lieutenant-Governor and the radical William Aberhart. Just over a year earlier, the Premier had thrown the

(Provincial Archives of Alberta, A.4940)

### Lieutenant-Governor Prevails
His Honour John Bowen, carrying his hat at the right of the photograph, insisted that an Alberta girl present flowers to Queen Elizabeth rather than Premier Aberhart's grand-daughter from Vancouver

Lieutenant-Governor out of Government House and closed the Vice-regal home as a cost cutting measure. With the enmity between the two men still souring their relationship, the Lieutenant-Governor and his Premier scrapped over every detail of the visit of the King and Queen. Aberhart chose his granddaughter from Vancouver to present a bouquet to the Queen on behalf of the province of Alberta.[79] In a flash of common sense, she was replaced at the last minute by a local Alberta girl, much to the pleasure of the Lieutenant-Governor.[80]

Following the provincial government reception in the Legislature, their Majesties proceeded to the Lieutenant-Governor's suite of offices for tea. As the royal couple passed through the doors of the suite, His Honour closed them in the face of Premier Aberhart and his wife who were left standing in embarrassment before reporters. The Canadian Prime Minister, Mackenzie King, who was accompanying their Majesties across Canada was told by the Lieutenant-Governor that he simply "had to limit the numbers". Not accepting this explanation, Mackenzie King changed the Lieutenant-Governor's plans by returning to the corridor outside the Lieutenant-Governor's office and taking the Premeir and his wife by the arms, and leading them into the Vice-regal suite for refreshments.[81]

The official state dinner went off well except that the Bowen's decided to leave even before the King and Queen because, Bowen complained, the Aberharts dominated conversation with the royal couple. In the end, Mackenzie King persuaded the Bowens to remain for some final words with the King and Queen. Then the Canadian Prime Minister discovered that the

160

*Premier Prevails at State Dinner*

(Provincial Archives of Alberta, A.2047)

While the Aberharts dominated conversation at the Provincial State Dinner in the Macdonald Hotel and Mrs. Edith Bowen conversed with Canadian Prime Minister Mackenzie King, His Honour John Bowen is left to look out over the dinner guests at the right of the picture

Lieutenant-Governor and his wife had no transportation—Aberhart had cut their chauffeured-driven vehicle from public expense accounts. Again, Mackenzie King rose to the occasion and helped to patch over the dispute between the Vice-regal representative and the Premier by offering the Bowens a lift to the station in his car for the final farewells to the royal guests.[82]

Other Royals arrived after World War II. On 27 October 1951, His Honour John Bowlen presided over a dinner for Princess Elizabeth and her husband, Prince Philip.[83] Later, during the 1959 visit to the capital on their

Majesties' cross-Canada tour, the Honourable John Bowlen hosted a garden party for The Queen on the Legislature grounds.

Sometimes royalty calls unexpectedly. In February 1963, His Honour Percy Page and his wife drove out to the Edmonton International Airport to greet Queen Elizabeth and Prince Philip who had been forced to land in Edmonton because of bad weather conditions in Vancouver.[84]

At a state dinner in honour of Her Majesty in 1973 at Calgary, the Honourable Grant MacEwan sat beside The Queen. He said later that "'Her Majesty is not one to make comments but is tireless in asking questions.'" He

(Glenbow Archives, NA2864-23296)

### Farewell
The Honourable Grant MacEwan and his wife Phyllis say farewell to Her Majesty Queen Elizabeth II at the end of her visit to Calgary in 1973

said that their conversational exchanges "'consisted at her questions and my replies as well as I could make them—mostly about Alberta.'"[85] He was far more keen on his chatting with the conservation-minded Prince Philip than the Queen.[86] During that visit to the province, Her Majesty had come to participate in events marking the Royal Canadian Mounted Police centennial.

Again in 1990, Queen Elizabeth II visited the province of Alberta. On 30 June, Her Majesty officially opened the Museum of the Regiments in Calgary and presented new colours to the Calgary Highlanders of which she is Colonel-in-chief. During this visit, she also granted the right to the Tyrrell Museum at Drumheller to use the title "Royal".[87] At the beginning of each of her visits, the Lieutenant-Governor has greeted Her Majesty upon her arrival in Alberta.

(City of Edmonton Archives, EA10-781)

*Greeting Princess Elizabeth* 1951
After greeting Princess Elizabeth at the railway station in Edmonton,
His Honour John Bowlen accompanies her to a waiting car,
followed by the Lieutenant-Governor's wife Caroline and Premier
Ernest Manning

(Provincial Archives of Alberta, A.12709)

*Princess Margaret Visit 1980*
His Honour Frank Lynch-Staunton greets Princess Margaret during her visit to help celebrate Alberta's 75th Anniversary

(Provincial Archives of Alberta, A.13960)

*The Queen Mother Visits Alberta 1985*
Her Honour Helen Hunley hosts the Queen Mother

(Michael Aporius, *The Edmonton Journal*)

## Earl and Countess of Wessex Visit Edmonton August 2001
Her Honour Lois Hole greets Prince Edward and Sophie, the Countess of Wessex, at the Edmonton International Airport. The royal couple came to attend the World Championships in Athletics

Besides acting as host to the Queen and other members of the Royal Family, the Lieutenant-Governor also greets the Governor General and entertains visiting heads of state and other official visitors to the province at dinners, luncheons and receptions.

(Glenbow Archives, ND-3-6968d)

Visit of Governor General Bessborough 1935
His Honour William Walsh greets Governor General Bessborough at Edmonton

(Provincial Archives of Alberta, A.13,969)

## Governor General Sauvé Visits Edmonton
Her Honour Helen Hunley greets Her Excellency Jeanne Sauvé

(Courtesy of the Office of the Secretary to the Governor General)

## Her Excellency Adrienne Clarkson Visits Edmonton 2000
His Honour H. A. Bud Olson greets Governor General Clarkson at Government House

Unveiling of Official Portrait

Since the 1970s, the Speaker of the Legislative Assembly has decided that outside the Lieutenant-Governor's office on the third floor of the Legislature Building, the portraits of all former Lieutenant-Governors of Alberta should be displayed. Over time, a special ceremony has developed to mark the unveiling of the official portrait of the Lieutenant-Governor shortly after the Queen's representative leaves office. The Speaker of the Legislative Assembly, who is responsible for all activity within the Legislature Building, presides over this event.

(Province of Alberta Archives, J.2071)

**Portrait Unveiling**
The portrait of the Honourable Percy Page was unveiled in the presence of family members Wednesday, 29 October 1975

Guests gather in the Confederation room on the third floor of the Legislature Building and are escorted in procession to the West Wing by the Sergeant-at-Arms of the Assembly where the ceremony occurs. After opening remarks by the Speaker, the Premier, Leader of the Official Opposition and the leader of any third party speaks. The former Lieutenant-Governor then unveils the official portrait[88] and offers a few remarks. The Speaker then closes the ceremony. A luncheon or dinner is then held where the Speaker presents the Lieutenant-Governor with a gift from the people of Alberta.

When His Honour Grant MacEwan retired from his Vice-regal post, the province possessed a portrait of His Honour painted by Illingworth Kerr in 1970. MacEwan himself was indifferent to the portrait, but the government did not approve of the likeness and commissioned Harley Brown to paint another.[89] The Brown portrait now hangs in its proper place outside the Lieutenant-Governor's office in the Legislature Building. Grant MacEwan was not present for its unveiling in 1982. The province, however, held a dinner in his honour in 1974 and presented him with a car. The next day he took the luxurious automobile to a dealer and exchanged it for a smaller model that would use less gasoline and be less gaudy. The savings he returned to the Alberta Treasury. This gesture was typical of the environmentally minded Grant MacEwan.

His Honour Ralph Steinhauer attended the unveiling of his portrait on 29 April 1983. His farewell dinner had been held a few years earlier when he left office in 1979. Because His Honour loved fishing, the province gave him a boat, motor and trailer, but no licence plate for the trailer of his parting gift.

### Rejected Portrait
This portrait of the Honourable Grant MacEwan by Illingworth Kerr was rejected by the government as His Honour's official portrait for unspecified reasons

### Official Portrait
The government commissioned Harley Brown to paint this official portrait of His Honour Grant MacEwan

No one explained how His Honour managed to get his equipment home from his farewell dinner at the Hotel Macdonald that evening![90]

At the time Her Honour Helen Hunley's portrait was unveiled on 26 April 1991, the Legislature was still in session. Thus, Her Honour was invited into the Legislative Chamber to speak before the ceremony itself. The government of Premier Don Getty established the "Helen Hunley Graduate Scholarship for Studies in Mental Health" to honour her. This gift was appropriate since the Honourable Helen Hunley had served as Alberta Minister of Social Services and Community Health and had chaired the Alberta Mental Health Advisory Council after leaving active politics.[91]

(Bruce Edwards, *The Edmonton Journal*)

*Portrait Unveiling*
Her Honour Helen Hunley looks at her portrait following the unveiling ceremony Friday, 26 April 1991

171

*Portrait Unveiling*
The Honourable Gordon Towers
helps to unveil his portrait
Monday, 17 June 1996

(Rick MacWilliam, *The Edmonton Journal*)

*Portrait Unveiling*
His Honour Bud Olson examines his portrait
after it was unveiled
Thursday, 23 November 2000

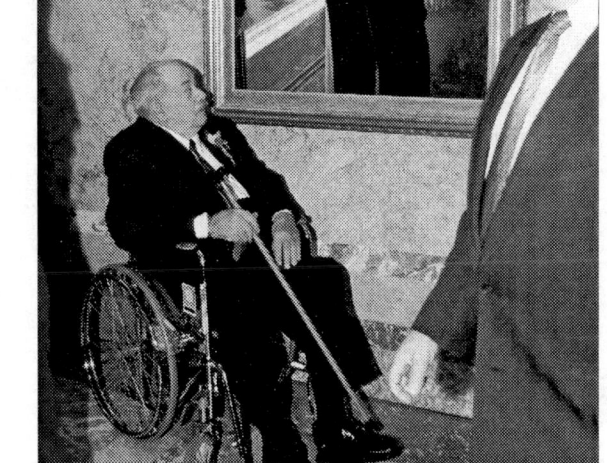

(Larry Wong, *The Edmonton Journal*)

When leaving office, each of the Lieutenant-Governors has been given a gift which has typified each one's "special interest" in some aspect of provincial life while acting as the Vice-royal representative for Alberta.

State Funerals

State Funerals are a right of passage (death) which the province began to mark when, for the first time in Alberta's history, a Lieutenant-Governor died while holding office. In the past seventy years, no coherent ceremonial language has emerged with respect to funerals since the taste for this specific type of royal ritual has escaped many of the holders of the Vive-regal office. The lying-in-state at the Legislature Building has allowed ordinary Albertans to pay tribute to the life and work of the deceased Lieutenant-Governor by filing past the coffin and signing a book of condolence. This ceremonial occurrence combined with the procession through the streets of Edmonton with the coffin placed on a gun carriage or in a hearse, followed by a more private interment, has become characteristic of these provincial state occasions. To give visible expression to solidarity with the past and continuity to the present, the incumbent holder of the office of Lieutenant-Governor is always present at the religious service and provincial flags are lowered to half-mast. This dignified ceremonial has rendered Vice-royal ritual both comforting and popular in our post-modern age where the attributes of continuity, uniqueness, tradition and permanence are often lacking.

## His Honour Philip Primrose (1936-37)

His Honour Philip Primrose was the first Lieutenant-Governor to die in office and was accorded Alberta's first state funeral. Following precedent established by Royal funerals held in Britain, the casket containing his body was taken to the Legislature for the laying-in-state on Friday, 19 March 1937. Standing rigid and silent resting with arms reverse, four constables of the Royal Canadian Mounted Police formed a guard of honour around the casket in front of the Speaker's rostrum. The desks of the Members of the Assembly were

(Provincial Archives of Alberta, Ks.12/1)

**Lying in State**
His Honour Philip Primrose lying in state in the Legislature
19 March 1937

draped in purple for the occasion as 1,800 Albertans filed by the flag-draped casket.[92] The body was returned to the funeral home from the Legislature and from there transferred to Government House on Saturday morning. At 3:00 PM, the casket was taken to First Presbyterian Church where the funeral service was conducted by Major D. F. Cameron, librarian of the University of Alberta, assisted by the Rev. Dr. Andrew Osborn of First Presbyterian Church.[93]

The chief mourners for this first state funeral in Alberta were the immediate family, government members, judiciary, military officers, consular corps, Royal North-West Mounted Police veterans, leaders of the opposition parties in the Legislature and other leading dignitaries from the city of Edmonton. Non-commissioned officers were in uniform recruited from various military units and acted as ushers in the church. The Speaker of the Assembly, the Honourable Peter Dawson attended in robes and tri-cornered hat, and the Sergeant-at-Arms, Captain H. S. Newby, and all military officers were present in uniform. The front of the church was banked high with floral tributes, including one from the Governor General, Lord Tweedsmuir.[94]

The band of the 49th Edmonton Regiment played en route to the Edmonton cemetery. People lined the streets of the capital to pay their last respects as the funeral procession proceeded from the church to the burial ground. As the procession left First Presbyterian Church, a salute was fired. There were 15 one-minute rounds fired by the 92nd Battery, Royal Canadian Artillery, from the Legislature Grounds. The grave side firing party which fired three rounds over the grave consisted of one sergeant, one corporal and 13 constables of the Royal Canadian Mounted Police.[95] This state funeral set the precedent for others in the future.

*His Honour John Bowlen (1950-1959)*

The second Lieutenant-Governor to be accorded a state funeral was His Honour John Bowlen, a Roman Catholic who died in office 16 December 1959. The four ranking officers of the armed services and the Royal Canadian Mounted Police in Edmonton formed the honour guard during the first 15 minutes in which the body of the Honourable John Bowlen lay in state in the Legislature Building.[96] He was buried out of the Roman Catholic Cathedral in Edmonton. There was a procession down Jasper Avenue after the

(Public Archives of Alberta, A 13.919)

**Lying in State**
The Lying in State of His Honour John Bowlen
18 December 1959

**Funeral Procession**
The funeral procession at the cemetery of His Honour John Bowlen
19 December 1959

high mass with the casket placed on a gun carriage and the Princess Patricia Canadian Light Infantry band playing with muffled drums. The state funeral was held Saturday, 19 December 1959 before the burial in St. Joachim's Cemetery in Edmonton.[97]

*His Honour Grant MacEwan (1966-1974)*

Although he did not die in office, a state funeral was held for His Honour Grant MacEwan. His body, in a white casket covered with the Canadian flag, lay in state before the grand staircase in the rotunda of the Legislature Building on Monday, 19 June 2000. The four member vigil guard

(Bruce Edwards, *The Edmonton Journal*)

### Lying in State
The Lying in State in the Rotunda of the Legislature
Building of His Honour Grant MacEwan
19 June 2000

was drawn from various members of the military and police force. Before the doors opened to the public, family and closest friends filed by the casket as did Her Honour Lois Hole, Premier Klein and other dignitaries.[98] The funeral service for Grant MacEwan took place at Robertson-Wesley United Church in Edmonton.[99]

*Other Vice-regal Funerals*

There was no state funeral for His Honour Percy Page when he died in March 1973, but the Premier, Peter Lougheed, Lieutenant-Governor Grant MacEwan and Mayor of Edmonton, Ivor Dent, attended the private service at Robertson-Wesley United Church. Also, surviving members of the Edmonton Grads Basketball Club were present on this solemn occasion.[100]

When Frank Lynch-Staunton died 25 September 1990, his funeral was held at Pincher Creek and a Memorial Service took place at Christ Church Cathedral on 2 October 1990 in Edmonton with the Lieutenant-Governor, Helen Hunley, present.[101] The family of His Honour Gordon Towers were asked if they wished a state funeral when he died on 8 June 1999, but the family declined the offer. Although His Honour "Bud" Olson requested a private family funeral, the Lieutenant-Governor, provincial and federal government representatives, as well as the South Alberta Light Horse who formed an honour guard were present at his funeral in Medicine Hat, 18 February 2002.[102] In Alberta, the tradition has developed that Lieutenant-Governors be accorded a state funeral if their families so desire.

Whether for funerals, the unveiling of an official portrait, the swearing in of Members of the Legislative Assembly and provincial Privy Council Members, the Opening of the provincial Legislature or the installation of a Lieutenant-Governor, the province of Alberta has developed state ceremonies focusing on the Vice-regal representative of the Queen which dignifies these occasions with appropriate pomp and circumstance to symbolize for Albertans their civic society under a constitutional Monarchy.

## NOTES

1. Barbara Dacks, "Her Honour Lois Hole, Alberta's New Lieutenant-Governor speaks her mind and follows her heart", *Legacy*, (fall 2000), 32.

2. Interview with Shelagh Rogers on This *Morning* (CBC Radio One), 20 May 2002 (Victoria Day). See also *Edmonton Senior*, Vol. 12, No. 10, July 2002, 1 & 15.

3. *Edmonton Journal,* Tuesday, 6 April 2004, B4.

4. *Edmonton Journal,* Tuesday, 6 April 2004, B4.

5. *Edmonton Journal,* 10 February 2000.

6. *Edmonton Sun,* Friday, 2 May 2004, 6. (Column by Graham Hicks)

7. Barbara Dacks, "Her Honour Lois Hole, Alberta's New Lieutenant-Governor speaks her mind and follows her heart", *Legacy*, (fall 2000), 32.

8. Dr. Maxwell Foran, "Excerpt from the eulogy to former Lieutenant-Governor Grant MacEwan", *Legacy*, (fall 2000), 3.

9. *Calgary Herald*, 23 February 1991.

10. Tony Cashman, *The Best Edmonton Stories,* Edmonton: Hurtig Publishers, [1976], 202.

11. Edmonton *Journal,* 2 September 1905; a good description is provided in James G. MacGregor, *A History of Alberta*, Edmonton: Hurtig Publishers, [1972], 189.

12. *Edmonton Journal*, 20 & 21 October 1915.

13. *Edmonton Journal*, 30 October 1925.

14. *Calgary Herald*, Friday 16 October 1936, 1.

15. *Edmonton Journal*, Friday 16 October 1936, 14.

16. H. Blair Neatby, *William Lyon Mackenzie King: The Lonely Heights 1924-1932*. [Toronto]: University of Toronto Press, [1963], 63.

17. *Edmonton Journal,* Friday, 30 October 1925, 8. See also *Calgary Herald,* Thursday, 29 October 1925, 11.

18. Roger Graham, *Arthur Meighen: And Fortune Fled*, Vol. II. Toronto: Clarke, Irwin & Col, 1963, 354.

19. For a very good brief account of this case see Brian Brennan, "Emilio 'Emperor Pic' Picariello and Florence Lassandro" in Brian Brennan, *Scoundrels and Scallywags*, [Calgary]: Fifth House, [2003], 51-63.

20. *Edmonton Journal,* Friday, 14 January 1936, 1-2.

21. *Edmonton Journal,* 6 May 1931.

22. *Edmonton Journal,* Friday 14 January 1936, 1-2.

23. *Edmonton Journal,* 1 October 1936.

24. *Ibid.*

25. *Edmonton Bulletin,* 17 March 1937.

26. *Edmonton Journal,* 23 March 1937.

27. Provincial Archives of Alberta, tape of conversation with Mrs. J. C. (Oliver) Bowen, recorded 27 March 1972, #72.128.

28. *Ibid.*

29. *Edmonton Journal,* 1 February 1950.

30. *Edmonton Journal,* Wednesday, 16 March 1960.

31. Harold Hilliard, "He's a Vice-regal cowboy" in *Star Weekly,* 20 August 1955, 7.

32. Frank Dolphin, *The Alberta Legislature: A Celebration,* Edmonton: Plains Publishing Inc., 1987, 53.

33. *Edmonton Journal,* 21 December 1959 & 22 December 1959.

34. *Edmonton Journal,* 2 January 1966.

35. *Edmonton Journal,* 22 June 2000, A17.

36. *Ibid.*

37. *Edmonton Journal,* 2 July 1974.

38. *Edmonton Journal,* 3 July 1974.

39. *Edmonton Journal,* 19 October 1979.

40. *Edmonton Journal*, 23 January 1985.

41. *Edmonton Sun,* Sunday 19 February 1989, Comment & Lifestyle, 1.

42. *Ibid.*

43. *Edmonton Journal*, 31 December 1990, 1.

44. *Edmonton Sun,* Sunday, 19 February 1989, Copmment & Lifestyle, 1.

45. *Edmonton Journal*, 12 march 1991.

46. *Ibid.*

47. *Edmonton Journal*, 10 June 1999, A5.

48. *Ibid.*

49. *Ibid.*

50. Mary Janigan, "A super-minister at home on the range" in *Macleans,* 12 April 1982, Vol. 95, No. 15, 12,16 & 20.

51. Lorne Gunter, "The Senator wielded clout" in Edmonton *Journal,* Sunday, 17 February 2002, A14.

52. *Edmonton Journal*, 18 April 1996.

53. *Edmonton Journal*, 11 February 2000. Column by Nick Lees, B1.

54. *Edmonton Journal*, 10 February 2000.

55. *Edmonton Journal*, 11 February 2000. Column by Nick Less, B1.

56. *Edmonton Journal*, 11 February 2000.

57. *Edmonton Journal*, 11 February 2000. Nick Less column, B1.

58. *Ibid.*

59. Gordon Barnhart, "The Queen in Saskatchewan", *Canadian Parliamentary Review,* 10.4 (Winter 1987-8), 14.

60. Moragh Macauley, "Alberta's Legislative Building", *Canadian Parliamentary Review,* 10.3 (autumn 1987), 7.

61. *Edmonton Journal,* 30 January 1998.

62. Gary Garrison and Brian Hodgson, "Alberta's Black Rod: A gift of service and Commonwealth unity", *The Parliamentarian,* (April 1998), 199.

63. *Ibid.*

64. *Ibid.*

65. Frank Lynch-Staunton, *Greener Pastures: The Memoirs of F. Lynch-Staunton,* Edmonton: Jasper Printing Group, 1987, 38.

66. Douglas, J. Blain, "Symbols of Sovereignty", *Canadian Parliamentary Review* 4 (1981-82), 21-22.

67. Lynch-Staunton, *Greener Pastures,* 38.

68. *Edmonton Journal,* 14 February 1952.

69. *Ibid.,* 38.

70. *Edmonton Journal,* Friday 27 May 1910, 4.

71. *Calgary Herald,* 14 February 1996.

72. *Edmonton Sun,* 14 February 1996, 3.

73. *Edmonton Journal,* 30 January 1998.

74. David Elliott and Iris Miller, *Bible Bill: A Biography of William Aberhart,* [Edmonton]: Reidmore Books, [1987], 292.

75. *Edmonton Journal,* 12 July 1974, 39.

76. *Edmonton Journal,* 27 December 1950.

77. *Edmonton Journal,* 19 May 1993.

78. *Ibid.*

79. Tom MacDonnell, *Daylight Upon Magic: The Royal Tour of Canada —1939,* Toronto: Macmillan, [1989], 163.

80. *Ibid.,* 166.

81. *Ibid.,* 167.

82. *Ibid.,* 168.

83. *Edmonton Journal,* 5 October 1951.

84. *Edmonton Journal,* 1 February 1963.

85. R.H. Macdonald, *Grant MacEwan: No Ordinary Man,* Saskatoon: Western Producer Prairie Books, [1979], 242.

86. Donna von Hauff, *Everyone's Grandfather: The Life & Times of Grant MacEwan,* [Edmonton]: [Grant MacEwan Community College Foundation/Quon Editions], [1994], 153.

87. *Calgary Herald,* Wednesday 27 June 1990, A18 & 2 July 1990, A8.

88. These official portraits can been viewed in the Legislature Building or in the publication *Lieutenant-Governors of the Northwest Territories and Alberta 1876-1991,* Edmonton: Alberta Legislature Library, 1991.

89. Letter from Max Foran to Kenneth Munro, 7 June 2002 in the recipient's personal collection. Although the MacEwan family admired Kerr immensely, they were not overly impressed with his portrait of the Honourable Grant MacEwan. One member of the family wrote that "The most positive thing I recall about that portrait was Kerr's amazing depiction of Grant's hands. Easily the best I have seen." (Letter via e-mail from Max Foran to Ken Munro, Thursday, 16 September 2004 in the recipient's personal collection.)

90. *Edmonton Journal,* 19 September 1979.

91. *Edmonton Journal,* 29 April 1991.

92. *Edmonton Journal,* 22 March 1937.

93. *Ibid.*

94. *Ibid.*

95. *Edmonton Journal,* 19 March 1937.

96. *Edmonton Journal,* 18 December 1959.

97. *Edmonton Journal,* 16 December 1959, 18 December 1959, 19 December 1959, and 21 December 1959.

98. *Edmonton Journal,* 20 June 2000.

99. *Edmonton Journal,* 21 June 2000.

100. *Edmonton Journal,* 2 March 1973 & 6 March 1973.

101. *Edmonton Journal,* 26 September 1990 & 28 October 1990.

102. *Edmonton Journal,* Tuesday, 19 February 2002, B6.

# V
# OFFICIAL PUBLIC YEARLY CALENDAR OF THE LIEUTENANT-GOVERNOR

The Crown performs valuable symbolic functions on behalf of the people. These ceremonies are enhanced by the history, tradition, pageantry and majesty associated with the Monarch. The colour, stately and splendid display are decorative functions which help make citizens feel part of a community and express collection emotion and national pride. In Alberta, the Lieutenant-Governor as the Queen's representative fulfils the mandate of the Crown to symbolize, unify and personify the entire province through public celebrations. Some of these ceremonial occasions occur regularly each year on specific dates, while others are more tied to seasons rather than a definitive calendar date. The first such event which occurs at the very beginning of each calendar year is the New Year's Levee.

The New Year's Levee

The New Year's Levee began during the French Regime in Canada. The first confirmed occasion for this event took place in 1646. The Superior of the Jesuits wrote of 1 January 1646: "The soldiers went with their guns to salute Monsieur the Governor; and so did also the inhabitants in a body."[1] This tradition continued through the British regime to the present. In Alberta, this annual occasion which allows ordinary people to meet their sovereign or her representative began on 1 January 1907 shortly after the creation of the province on 1 September 1905.

In 1907, the levee was largely attended by gentlemen of Edmonton and Strathcona. His Honour George Bulyea, wearing the uniform of his high office, received in the cheerful drawing room of Government House. Callers were met at the door by his male secretary.[2] Then, in 1908, the officers of the Canadian Mounted Rifles attended the Lieutenant-Governor who received callers in the handsome reception room.[3] In 1909, His Honour held his levee in a suite of reception rooms while his wife, Annie Bulyea, received in the private parlour.[4] By 1911, the New Year's Levee was apparently "a social event of more than customary magnitude."[5] Generally, for this occasion the "reception parlours were very tastefully decorated with choice cut flowers and plants."[6] Naturally, when the new Government House was completed, the New Year's Levee followed the Lieutenant-Governor into his new residence.

In the years that followed his installation, His Honour William Egbert received with the Premier on the main floor of Government House while Her Honour Eva Egbert received upstairs.[7] The Walsh's continued this tradition.[8] One of the largest levee's was held in 1935 when more than 800 paid an official call on the Lieutenant-Governor. On that occasion, the Premier, Gavin Reid, was the first to pay respects and then remained to greet guests with the Lieutenant-Governor.[9] The numbers of guests were similar the following year when the President of the University of Alberta, Dr. Robert C. Wallace, received with the Lieutenant-Governor.[10]

A modification in tradition occurred in 1937 because of the illness of Lieutenant-Governor Primrose. On that occasion, Her Honour Lily Primrose acted on her husband's behalf and received the well dressed male Edmontonians at Government House.[11] The last New Year's Levee at Government House for many years happened in 1938 when the new Lieutenant-Governor, John Bowen, received over 900 guests along with the University of Alberta President, Dr. WIlliam A. R. Kerr.[12]

Because the Lieutenant-Governor was forced out of Government House in May 1938, the New Year's Levee was moved to the Legislature Building.[13] Bowen received in the Legislative Assembly Chamber in 1939[14] and again in 1940 when more than 1,100 persons attended.[15] Because of the difficulties of the War in 1942, no levee was held. However, in 1943, the Lieutenant-Governor received 400 Canadian and American military personnel. As a gesture of friendship, he also extended an invitation to the American Consul in Edmonton to receive with him.[16]

At the first levee held after the War, visitors walked up the main marble stairs of the Legislature Building flanked by the scarlet coated members of the Royal Canadian Mounted Police and into the Assembly Chamber to be received by His Honour John Bowen, and the Premier, Ernest Manning.[17] Because of the illness of Lieutenant-Governor Bowen in 1950, the New Year's Levee was not held; rather the Premier gave a reception in the Speaker's quarters of the Legislature Building.[18] The Edmonton historian, Tony Cashman, claims that by 1950 the New Year's Levee had dwindled to a "token observance" and required the enthusiasm of the next Lieutenant-Governor, John Bowlen, to restore the event to its traditional size and vitality.[19] By 1953, 1,000 army, navy and air force personnel along with members of the Royal Canadian Mounted

Police, Members of the Legislative Assembly, cabinet ministers, deputy ministers, civic officials, clergymen and others passed through the flag-bedecked doorway of the Legislative Chambre to be greeted by the Lieutenant-Governor and Premier[20] at this male-only affair.[21]

Another deviation from the norm occurred in 1957 when the Lieutenant-Governor received more than 1,400 men in the Legislative Assembly Chamber. That year, the Levee was held in two sessions; one for the military and the other for the general public. Two Hungarian refugees who had arrived in Edmonton following the abortive Hungarian Revolution of 1956 were presented to His Honour.[22] Because of the sudden death of the Lieutenant-Governor 16 December 1959, no Levee was held in 1960.[23] The next Lieutenant-Governor, Percy Page, continued the tradition of a male-only levee, but with a slight variation. In 1964 the military ranks were dotted with females from the three branches of the armed forces and one female civilian, the Belgian Vice-Consul in Edmonton.[24] Following past practice, no ordinary Albertan female civilians were allowed at these levees.

Despite all attempts to maintain this practice, during the New Year's Levee of 1965 a woman invaded the male sanctum! Louise Petty broke an age-old tradition by showing up at the Legislature to shake the hand of the Lieutenant-Governor. She claimed that the thought never crossed her mind that she was doing anything untoward. "This is the only time of the year we have the opportunity to pay homage to the Queen" she said. "I think everybody should be able to go."[25] A spokesman for the Lieutenant-Governor explained to the press that the Alberta tradition was to have men only at the Levee, but women, *properly dressed,* could visit with the Lieutenant-Governor and thus Louis Petty was admitted to the Levee.[26] Louise Petty's attendance, however, was considered an exception to a well defined rule of conduct for levees; women were simply not welcome.

In 1966, the Lieutenant-Governor designate, Grant MacEwan, attended the last Levee given by His Honour Percy Page.[27] In 1967 for his first New Year's Levee as Lieutenant-Governor, His Honour Grant MacEwan was assisted by Premier Ernest Manning and the President of the University of Alberta, Walter Johns. Again, the only females present were members of the armed forces.[28]

(Provincial Archives of Alberta, PA.675/2)

**New Year's Levee**
Grant MacEwan, Lieutenant-Governor designate, attends
the last New Year's Levee hosted by His Honour Percy Page
1966

(Provincial Archives of Alberta, J.408)

*New Year's Levee*
His Honour Grant MacEwan receives at the New Year's Levee

When Peter Lougheed became Premier of Alberta in 1971, he encouraged the Lieutenant-Governor to begin using Government House once again for this event. Lieutenant-Governor Ralph Steinhauer received there in 1975,[29] but because of repairs to Government House, the New Year's Levee returned to the Legislature Building for 1976 only.[30]

In 1978, a major change occurred with women admitted to the levee officially for the first time in Alberta's history. His Honour Ralph Steinhauer greeted 300 members of the Canadian Armed Forces, Royal Canadian Mounted Police, city policy, consular corps and the general public in the elegant dining room of Government House. His Honour wore a formal swallow-tail coat with a grey vest and matching trousers. The names of the guests were announced, hands shaken and then guests moved into a reception area where glasses of medium-dry sherry were handed out from large trays. After greeting all of his guests individually, His Honour mingled with Albertans, both male and female, who had come to meet him under the chandeliers of the dining room. In Ottawa, the tradition of having only men presented to the Crown's representative had been broken in 1976 when Governor General Jules Leger invited women to his New Year's Levee for the first time. The Lieutenant-Governor of Alberta embraced this new tradition two years later![31]

By 1981, His Honour Frank Lynch-Staunton invited children to join their parents at the annual New Year's Levee. That year, young Adrian Broonfield expressed his excitement on meeting the Lieutenant-Governor face to face for the first time.[32] Chatting to a reporter amid the trappings of high office at Government House during the Levee in 1985, one Edmonton woman sighed that "It's nice once a year to go first class". After signing the register, handing an introductory card to a military aide, members of the public were presented to the Lieutenant-Governor. Eggnog and hors-d'oeuvres were served and people were free to explore Government House.[33]

Many of the 400 who attended the Levee given by Her Honour Helen Hunley in 1987 were children. She said that the Levee was important to her "personally because I believe strongly in tradition...."[34]

Under His Honour Gordon Towers, another slight change occurred in the Levee; the Lieutenant-Governor now received with his wife. In 1996, the

(Courtesy of Lt Col Frank Kozar, Edmonton)

### 1991 Levee
Her Honour Helen Hunley, accompanied by her Aide-de-Camp, preparing to receive at the New Year's Levee at Government House

*(Courtesy of Lt Col Frank Kozar, Edmonton)*

**1995 Levee**
His Honour Gordon Towers and Mrs. Doris Towers prepare to receive at the New Year's Levee

Towers offered an assortment of baked goodies, moose milk, tea, coffee and Alberta roast hip of beef on a bun.  Within the first half hour, over 500 Albertans had come through the door out of the weather which was hovering at the freezing mark.[35]

The change in venue of the Levee in 1997 caused a nasty little spat between the former Lieutenant-Governor Gordon Towers and His Honour "Bud" Olson.  At the annual get-together in the fall of 1996 between the Governor General and Lieutenant-Governors, there was general consensus that by moving the New Year's Levee from time to time out of the capital city in each jurisdiction, the Crown could strengthen the personal and living bond between the Vice-regal representatives and the people. In response to this suggestion, His Honour "Bud" Olson decided to move the Levee from Edmonton to Medicine Hat for 1 January 1997. An un-decorous verbal quarrel erupted between His Honour and his predecessor. Gordon Towers "slammed" the move because it was a break with tradition and said the Levee should remain in Edmonton.[36] He called it a silly move and offered to tackle Olson "any time, anywhere" over the issue. Olson replied in his best provincial "royal" dialect, saying he did not "give a damn" what Towers thought.[37] Towers replied by calling on the Governor General to remove Olson from his Vice-regal post for "breaching tradition and using bad language."[38] Olson shrugged off that suggestion as "just a little silly."[39]

Ordinary Albertans joined in the fray over the location of the New Year's Levee. Major Keith Wakefield, a former aide-de-camp to Lieutenant-Governor Percy Page insisted that "the levee is a capital city activity." Although Percy Page was a teetotaller and did not want to serve moose milk (rum and egg-nog), he respected tradition, and decided "tradition should override his own feelings..."[40] and served alcoholic beverages at the function. If Percy Page could follow tradition, why could Olson not do the same, he wondered? Some Canadian Armed Forces personnel felt snubbed by the move because Edmonton was such a garrison town and hundreds of military members attended the annual event. Olson replied that he made the move to allow other Albertans to enjoy the reception.[41] As the representative of the Crown in Alberta, Olson felt strongly that everyone throughout the province had a right to see and talk to him.[42] Jim Horseman, a former provincial cabinet minister who had represented Medicine Hat in the Legislative Assembly explained that Olson was "trying to reach out with the office and make it more meaningful to all people."[43] An *Edmonton Journal* editorial writer agreed that "Any opportunity to enhance the profile of the Lieutenant-Governor by allowing for opportunities for Albertans to meet the incumbent should be welcomed." This move would serve to underscore the important position of our constitutional Monarch. However, the writer continued: " The Lieutenant-Governor should not tamper with the ritual of the Levee and its traditional link with Government House, but rather should establish a second annual ceremonial occasion, one which could move about the province from year to year."[44]

This idea which was also suggested by a member of the Monarchist League of Canada[45] was far more sensible than the uninformed utterances of Lorne Taylor, a Member of the Legislative Assembly. He used the occasion to denounce the Crown by asserting that "I don't think we need...[a Lieutenant-Governor]...They live off the expense of the Alberta taxpayer. Quite frankly, I don't think it's a necessary office."[46] The unseemly Olson-Towers tussle ended by 7 December 1996 when His Honour closed the debate on a Calgary radio talk show by informing the host that he refused to "duke it out" with Towers.[47]

In the end, the New Year's Levee took place without a hitch in Medicine Hat. One citizen, in a letter to the editor wrote that people lined up to shake hands with the Lieutenant-Governor, children gawked at the Royal Canadian Mounted Police officer in red serge and the public milled about, nibbling on free snacks of finger sandwiches, pastry squares and sliced fruit which was washed down by an non-alcoholic punch. It was noted that there were more cowboy boots at this Levee than at any former one![48] In 1998, His Honour, "Bud" Olson returned the Levee to Edmonton, but the following year, he held it in Calgary. In 2000, because of "Y2K jitters", no Levee was held.[49] That year many of the police and military officers who normally attended were on call in case of disaster.[50]

(John Lucas, *The Edmonton Journal*)

### 2001 Levee
The line of people waiting to meet Her Honour Lois Hole stretches for several hundred meters outside Government House on the occasion of her first New Year's Levee

Apparently, Her Honour Lois Hole has accepted the advice of the *Journal* editorial writer and decided to hold her New Year's Levees at Government House in Edmonton[51] with the promise of other receptions around the province on other occasions.[52] Her first Levee was an splendid success as over 2,000 Albertans made their way into the stately old mansion overlooking the river to greet the Crown's Alberta representative in the two hours set aside for the purpose. The subsequent Levee's have been equally successful.

(Courtesy of Lt Col Frank Kozar, Edmonton)

*New Year's Levee 2002*
Her Honour Lois Hole greets Lt Col Frank Kozar at Government House

## Victoria Day

Following the New Year's Levee, the next fixed occasion on the calendar year is the celebration of the "official" birthday of the Sovereign. Through Royal Proclamation in 1957,[53] Victoria Day has been appointed as the Sovereign's official birthday in Canada. It is celebrated each year as a public holiday across Canada and occurs on the Monday immediately preceding 25 May.

Victoria Day had its origins in the aftermath of the burning of the Parliament Buildings by the Tory mob in 1849 and the petition advocating annexation to the United States by respected Canadian businessmen following Royal Assent given to the "Rebellion Loses Bill" of the same year. As the century progressed, it expanded throughout the country and become a national legal holiday following the death of Queen Victoria in 1901 through an Act of Parliament.

In modern times, Victoria Day is seen as a publicly sanctioned occasion for private leisure and recreation. Generally, Canadians observe the holiday at beaches, opening cottages, planting gardens or watching sports events. One tradition has prevailed: to mark the Sovereign's birthday, a royal 21-gun salute is fired at noon on Victoria Day at the Legislature grounds.

Gradually, the day has become open to other formal events to mark the Sovereign's birthday. In 2001, for example, Her Honour Lois Hole presented medals during celebrations at the Legislature Grounds to peacekeepers who had done tours of duty in Bosnia, the Golan Heights, Cyprus, Egypt and other trouble spots. She also presented 12-year service medals and made a few promotions official. Dressed in black and wearing pearls, Her Honour greeted many who showed up to hear the 21-gun salute with handshakes and hugs.[54]

(Ed Kaiser, *The Edmonton Journal*)

*Victoria Day 2001*
At the Victoria Day Salute on the Legislature Grounds, Her Honour Lois Hole awarded former Lieutenant Foss Tackaberry an honourary appointment to Captain
(in 1939, Tackaberry, a gunner, fired a salute when King George VI visited Edmonton)

In 2002, the 20th Field Regiment Royal Canadian Artillery and the Royal Canadian Artillery Band assisted in the Victoria Day Salute celebrating the Golden Jubilee of Queen Elizabeth II. Her Honour Lois Hole fired the first round of the 21-gun Royal Salute to mark the Golden Jubilee. She also made presentations of medals and decorations, cut the Queen's birthday cake and

## Golden Jubilee Victoria Day

Her Honour Lois Hole Fires the first cannon for the Victoria Day Salute, 20 May 2002

Her Honour Lois Hole gives her traditional warm hug to a soldier on Victoria Day 20 May 2002

(Courtesy of Lt Col Frank Cozar, Edmonton)

(Courtesy of Lt Col Frank Kozar, Edmonton)

*Golden Jubilee Victoria Day*
Her Honour Lois Hole cuts Her Majesty The Queen's Golden Jubilee cake on Victoria Day, 20 May 2002

made a walk-about following the formal ceremonies. Albertans enjoyed the static displays manned by the members of the 20th Field Regiment Royal Canadian Artillery while the Royal Canadian Artillery Band performed. Under Lois Hole, the marking of the Sovereign's official birthday in Canada is becoming a formalized Vice-regal occasion of celebration on the grounds of the Alberta Legislature.

Canada Day

The Alberta Lieutenant-Governor also returns to the Alberta Legislature Grounds for the official celebrations of Canada Day on 1 July each year. Since the Diamond Jubilee of Confederation in 1927, Dominion Day, now called Canada Day since 1980, has become a great national festival devoted to patriotic rituals. Before 1927, it had been observed indifferently, eclipsed in British Canada by Victoria Day and in French Canada by St. Jean Baptiste Day.[55] In recent times, the Lieutenant-Governor participates in ceremonies at the provincial Legislature granting Canadian citizenship to newcomers and is present for the Canada Day Gun Salute. After taking the oath of citizenship before citizenship judge Gurcharan Singh Bhatia on the lawn of the Legislature 1 July 2002, sixty-four new Canadians from thirty-one different countries received the Vice-regal "hug" from Her Honour. The Lieutenant-Governor spoke with emotion as she explained to the hundreds of Canadians attending this moving ceremony that "citizenship is about 'pulling together for a better Canada....'" and that "Canadians share a firm commitment to the common good."[56] Such occasions reinforce the living bond between subject and sovereign.

Remembrance Day

The fourth calendar-specific official public function of the Lieutenant-Governor centres on Remembrance Day. In modern times, Remembrance Day is an important ceremonial royal occasion in Canada. It dates back to the early twentieth century and grew out of the devastation of the First World War. On the morning of 11 November 1918, at Mons in Belgium where Britain had entered the active campaign in 1914, Canada's 7th Infantry Brigade composed of the 42nd, 49th Edmonton and Princess Patricia Canadian Light Infantry recaptured the town from the Germans and swept on for seven miles by 11 o'clock when word flashed around the world that the War was over and the Armistice signed.[57]

After the Great War, mourning for the war dead did not, however, lead to a return to the excesses of Victorian mourning customs.[58] Where traditional ceremony seemed inadequate in the face of so much death and bereavement, alternate attempts to render such loses bearable were made in official, public formal ways. These attempts can be seem in the construction of war memorials and the evolution of the ritual of Armistice, later, Remembrance Day.[59] Armistice Day became a tribute by the living to the dead and the Cenotaph symbolized the empty tomb.[60] The two minutes of silence made public and corporate those persistent feelings of grief and sorrow. After World War I, millions of bereaved family members wanted some ceremony, some reassurance that their loved ones were not forgotten and had not died in vain.[61]

The Lieutenant-Governor was not publicly involved with remembrance in the few years immediately following the end of hostilities. In 1919, Armistice Day was celebrated quietly in Edmonton by the raising of the honour flag at city hall accompanied by two minutes of silence.[62] The following year, two minutes of silence were observed at noon by all city departments and the switch at the power house was pulled so that everything, including street cars, stopped for those two minutes. There was no particular ceremony in the years immediately following the Great War.[63]

*The Poppy Campaign*

Gradually, however, new traditions were invented to remind people of those who had sacrificed so very much. In 1921, the poppy was introduced into Canada and worn by 16,000 people.[64] In the Orient, the poppy was the flower of forgetfulness, a reference to the trance derived from the opium which can be distilled from the flower. Within the European tradition, the poppy came to signify remembrance after the Napoleonic wars which saw it spring into life on the former fields of battle once the fallen had been buried. A century later, a Canadian, Lieutenant-Colonel John McCrae, was one of the soldiers who noted this phenomenon and witnessed the scarlet poppies spring from the scorched earth between the graves of the dead in Flanders during the First World War. He immortalized the poppy in his poem *In Flanders' Field,* and because it seemed as if Nature herself bled for the sacrifice of men, the poppy came to symbolize the covering of the scars of battle and the promise of a better day.[65] The Great War Veterans Association adopted the idea of wearing the poppy upon the suggestion by a French woman, Madame Guerin. Thus, on Armistice Day in 1921, poppies made by the women and children of France were distributed in Canada for the first time.[66] Indeed, in recognizing the service of Canadian men and women to our country through their participation in the Armed Forces of Canada and as a gesture of remembrance, the federal government has printed McCrae's poem on the new $10.00 bills issued in 2001.

On Armistice Day in 1922, a scarlet poppy was placed on the grave of every man in Edmonton who had served during the Great War as a token of thanks for giving their lives for King and country.[67] In the modern era, a few weeks before each Remembrance Day, the Poppy Fund Campaign of the Royal Canadian Legion officially begins its fund-raising drive by presenting the Governor General with a poppy. A similar event is then held in each provincial capital at which the Lieutenant-Governors are presented with poppies to inaugurate the campaign at the provincial level.[68]

The official Poppy Drive of the Alberta-North West Territories Command of the Royal Canadian Legion occurred 28 October 1999. In the solemn dignity of the Legislature rotunda surrounded by the display overhead of the Regimental Colours of many of Alberta's historic military units, the Lieutenant-Governor, His Honour H. A. "Bud" Olson was presented with the first poppy at 11:00 AM. Flanked by senior members of the Alberta government and opposition parties on his right and the members of the Alberta-North West Territories Command and Ladies Auxiliary on his left, and backed by the

Legislature Sergeant-at-Arms Brian Hodgson, His Honour commended the Legion for its work for veterans and the cause of remembrance by insisting "'the dead of war will not be forgotten, nor will their sacrifice have been made in vain.'"[69] This tradition of the Alberta-North West Territories Command of the Royal Canadian Legion presenting the Lieutenant-Governor with the first poppy in launching its annual Poppy Campaign has become an important event in the calendar of the Vice-regal representative in Alberta each year as a supplement to the ritual of Remembrance Day itself.[70]

*Poppy Ceremony in Legislature Rotunda*

(Courtesy of Rod Stewart, Royal Canadian Legion, Alberta-N.W.T Command)

His Honour Bud Olson speaks after receiving the first poppy
October 1998

(Courtesy of Rod Stewart, Royal Canadian Legion, Alberta-N.W.T Command)

His Honour Bud Olson receives the first poppy
1999

(Courtesy of Rod Stewart, Royal Canadian Legion, Alberta-N.W.T Command)

Her Honour Lois Hole pinning on the first poppy
2000

(Courtesy of Rod Stewart, Royal Canadian Legion, Alberta-N.W.T Command)

Her Honour Lois Hole greets participants at "First Poppy Ceremony", 2000

*Annual Remembrance Day Service*

Ceremonial surrounding 11 November has changed with time. From 1923 to 1931, the Canadian government decided to merge Armistice Day and Thanksgiving Day. In addition, as the public's desire heightened to make certain that young Canadians had not died in vain, the Lieutenant-Governor of Alberta became more involved in the ceremony of remembrance. In 1924, Lieutenant-Governor Brett attended the Armistice Service at Memorial Hall under the auspices of the Great War Veterans' Association.[71] Because the following year he left Edmonton on the evening of 11 November 1925 as his term of office had been completed, the mayor presided over the Memorial Service in Edmonton.[72] The following year, the Lieutenant-Governor attended services at Memorial Hall under the auspices of the newly formed Canadian Legion.[73]

As time past, attempts were made to bring more uniformity into ceremonies surrounding Armistice Day. In 1927, in conformity with the wishes expressed by His Majesty the King, Canadians everywhere interrupted their labours at 11 o'clock and stood in silence for two minutes as "a tribute of remembrance to the nation's 60,000 war dead and to those who still carry with them the ranks and scars of service."[74] The telephone was suspended; traffic was stopped whenever possible; magistrates and judges paused in the administration of justice; civic, government and commercial institutions halted their services to remember those "who had made the supreme sacrifice of life itself that right should triumph over might."[75] Nevertheless, until 1931 when federal government, through legislation, designated 11 November as

"Remembrance Day" in Canada, the Lieutenant-Governor did not attend memorial services as a "traditional duty" of the Crown. From that point on, however, the Crown's representatives were present at such ceremonies to represent all of the people within their respective jurisdictions.

In September 1936, Governor General Lord Tweedsmuir came to Edmonton to unveil the newly constructed cenotaph. Edmonton was one of the last cities in the Dominion to erect such a monument.[76] By 1936, on the 18th anniversary of the "11-11-11" Peace, the Dominion came to a pause, not to

(City of Edmonton Archives, EA-29-3)

### Edmonton's War Memorial Unveiled
Governor General Lord Tweedsmuir unveils Edmonton's War Memorial
September 1936

celebrate the victory, but to pay tribute to the 7,500,000 men of *all nations* whose lives were forfeited.[77] (This was also the year that King Edward VIII unveiled the Vimy Ridge monument at the sight of that horrendous battle of 1917.[78])

During the Second World War, Remembrance Day services continued. In 1942, His Honour John Bowen and the Premier, William Aberhart, attended the memorial service in the Canadian Legion Memorial Hall.[79]

By 1953, 5,000 people watched the Lieutenant-Governor deposite a wreath on behalf of all Albertans at the cenotaph as a tribute to the memory of those who died in the Two Great Wars and the Korean war. The Chaplain stressed the importance of remembering the cause for which they had made the supreme sacrifice.[80] The laying of a wreath and taking the salute of the Canadian Armed Forces and Veterans have become a recognized tradition for Lieutenant-Governors.[81]

A change of venue for the ceremony took place in 1978 because that June, the 65-ton cenotaph was moved from its original Bellamy Hill site at 100th avenue and 102nd street to City Hall.[82] When the weather became unbearable in 1987, the ceremony itself was moved, leaving the cenotaph behind in front of City Hall. The freezing temperatures through the 1970s and 1980s hampered the ceremonial pageantry of the Remembrance Day Services, particularly as musical instruments ceased to perform properly. The wise decision to move the ceremony indoors for the benefit of all came in 1986 when the mercury fell to -19 degrees Celsius and winds gusted to 35 kilometres an hour![83] To encourage greater public participation and give aging

(Provincial Archives of Alberta, J.4324/1)

*Remembrance Day Ceremony, 11 November 1978*
Lieutenant-Governor Ralph Steinhauer laid a wreath on behalf of all Albertans at the cenotaph in front of Edmonton's former City Hall.

veterans a more pleasant setting out of the increment weather, the ceremony was first moved indoors to the Kinsman Fieldhouse in 1987[84] and then more permanently to the University of Alberta "Butterdome" (Universiade Pavillion) the following year.[85] Following these ceremonies where wreaths were placed before a substitute cenotaph indoors, the wreaths were moved to the main cenotaph in front of City Hall.[86]

In 1990, with 4,500 gathered at the "Butterdome", Her Honour Helen Hunley reminded Albertans that "We do not come here to glorify war, we come in solemn remembrance to pay tribute to those who served." During the Second World War, Her Honour had dodged bombs as she put out spot fires near London's Hyde Park. Years later she remembered that a "lot of those bombs were uncomfortably close..."[87] Helen Hunley was not injured in the more than two years she served as an army administrator and instructor in Britain during the War, but because of that experience, Remembrance Day always had a very special significance for her. She stood proudly on a white podium possibly recalling personal experiences as legionnaires and members of the Canadian Armed Forces marched past her.[88] When asked about the observance of Remembrance Day, she replied that it was "still being treated with the same respect, but perhaps not with as much emotion..."[89] as in the immediate post-war period.

As with all ceremony and ritual, Remembrance Day has not been without controversy. Following the 1996 Remembrance Day Services, the former Lieutenant-Governor, Gordon Towers, criticized His Honour "Bud" Olson for his conduct at the event. Towers was peeved that Olson neglected to remove his old homburg during the playing of the anthems at the Service. He was furious that His Honour had turned up in a distinctly un-regal brown suit with a stumpy clip-on-tie and, according to Gordon Towers, had mumbled casually and inaudibly into the microphone. Towers insisted that "If he's not doing the job, he shouldn't be there." Olson, in a questionable royal rebuttal, flatly stated that Towers was a "lightweight" with "no influence on anybody that counts."[90] In more recent years, with her warmth and charm, Her Honour Lois Hole has placed Remembrance Day above petty comment.

Investitures and Award Ceremonies

Besides these fixed calendar functions such as Remembrance Day, the Lieutenant-Governor presides at other ceremonies throughout the calendar year which derive from the Crown's role as the font of all awards and honours. These marks of public regard symbolize the highest ideals of the people of Alberta and represent the community's thanks to the recipients for attaining them. To keep these cherished values before us, such ceremonies are held at regular, but not date specific, intervals.

*The Alberta Order of Excellence*

The investiture for the Alberta Order of Excellence normally occurs towards the end of October each year. Some of the noted individuals who have become members of the Alberta Order of Excellence include the Honourable Ernest Manning, the Honourable Grant MacEwan, Dr. Stanley A. Milner, Dr. Francis G. Winspear, Dr. Shirley M. Stinson and Louis Armand

Desrochers. At an impressive formal investiture ceremony at Government House on Thursday, 19 October 2000, Dr. Lorne Tyrrell of Edmonton was also welcomed as a member to the Order. The then Dean of Medicine at the University of Alberta, Dr. Lorne Tyrrell, is a noted researcher and specialist in infectious diseases who, with his team, discovered an antiviral therapy for the deadly liver disease, chronic hepatitis B. He is admired for his teaching abilities, his dedication to patients and his championing of developing quality medical health care in Alberta and Canada.[91]

In October 2000, Dr. Tyrrell received a message that the Lieutenant-Governor wished him to call her. Since Her Honour had broken her ankle a few months previously, he assumed that she was going to ask him to refer her to a bone specialist to obtain a second opinion about her injury which was apparently healing slowly. Dr. Tyrrell had had several conversations with Her Honour about medicine and specifically about Her Honour's ankle while she had served as Chancellor of the University of Alberta. Thus, he made a call to a specialist to make certain Her Honour would be able to see him and then he returned the Lieutenant-Governor's call. Dr. Tyrrell was taken aback when the Lieutenant-Governor did not wish to ask for advice about a bone specialist, but rather congratulated him on being made a member of the Alberta Order of Excellence. No one was more honoured or more surprised at this turn of events than the internationally acclaimed physician!

(Courtesy of Dr. Lorne Tyrell)

*Alberta Order of Excellence Ceremony*
Dr. Lorne Tyrell receives the Alberta Order of Excellence from Her Honour Lois Hole,
19 October 2000

*Queen's Counsel*

Besides the Alberta Order of Excellence Award presentation once a year, twice a year the Lieutenant-Governor appoints Queen's Counsels for Alberta. Ontario and Quebec have done away with the practice, but it is still followed in Alberta. Many complained that it was merely political patronage and thus in 2001 the system was changed to remove partisanship from the process. A committee that involves judges and the Law Society of Alberta does the initial screening of the proposed candidates. Nominees are selected for their significant contributions to the legal profession, to their communities or to legal scholarship. For example, in 2002, the Dean of the Faculty of Law at the University of Alberta, Lewis Klar, was appointed for his contribution in the latter category. He certainly felt that "It's an honour to those who receive them."[92]

(Courtesy of Gerald Robertson, Q.C.)

**Queen's Counsel Scroll**
The scroll received by Gerald Robertson upon his appointment as Queen's Counsel
(Note Lieutenant-Governor Bud Olson's signature at the top right hand corner of the scroll)

*The Order of St John of Jerusalem*

As Vice-Prior of the Most Venerable Order of St John of Jerusalem in Alberta, the Lieutenant-Governor presides over Investitures and confers the rank and insignia for each grade of the Order.

(Courtesy of Lt Col Frank Kozar, Edmonton)

**The Most Venerable Order of St John of Jerusalem Investiture Ceremony**
His Honour Bud Olson presided over an investiture ceremony of the Order of St John of Jerusalem, 6 November 1999

(Courtesy of Lt Col Frank Kozar, Edmonton)

## The Most Venerable Order of St John of Jerusalem
Constable Stewart Angus receives the Order of St John Life Saving Medal from Her Honour Lois Hole with the Honourable Ted Hole looking on

*The Duke of Edinburgh Awards*

Although not always called upon to preside over the ceremony awarding young people the Duke of Edinburgh Awards, the Lieutenant-Governor fills in for the Duke of Edinburgh if he himself, or another designated member of the Royal Family, are unable to present these awards in the province to the young recipients.

His Royal Highness, The Duke of Edinburgh initiated the Duke of Edinburgh's Award in 1956. He is the Founder and Patron of the Award which is "a voluntary, non-competitive programme of practical, cultural and adventurous activities, designed to support the personal and social development of young people aged 14-25."[93] The activities for this voluntary programme are carried out during the young person's free time. Award Groups are run by adults, many of whom are volunteers who share their skills, enthusiasm and organizing abilities to help young people reach their potential. There are three progressive levels---bronze, silver and gold—and four sections to the programme: service, skills, physical recreation and expeditions. The minimum time required to achieve the gold level would be approximately eighteen months. The Duke of Edinburgh has often come to Alberta for this award presentation, but the Lieutenant-Governor has also, on numerous occasions, presided over the award ceremony since its inception.

*Other Award Ceremonies*

The Lieutenant-Governor presides over other award ceremonies from time to time throughout the year such as those for the Royal Life Saving Society of Canada, Firefighter Service Awards, Police Awards and Military Awards.

(City of Edmonton Archives, EA20-872)

**Award Presentation Ceremony**
Lieutenant-Governor Ralph Steinhauer presents A. H. Savage with the
Alberta Lifesaving Award, 8 January 1975

Other Functions

In addition to focusing Albertans' attention of our most cherished ideals through investiture and award ceremonies, the Lieutenant-Governors continually enrich Canadian heritage. Through the person of the Lieutenant-Governor, the Crown is made visible among us. A public appearance by the Queen's representative in Alberta has a special meaning. It lends a sense of occasion to any circumstance or event, whether it be the full pageantry of arriving in a horse drawn carriage, the dedication of a public building, a visit to a camp for physically challenged children or the observance of a sporting event. The Lieutenant-Governor's attendance is a gesture that asks for no return and is a statement that the event is one which deserves wide attention by the whole province. Such visits remind all those who are present of a reality that is greater than each one of them, of the community symbolized by the Crown's representative.[94]

These functions attended by the Lieutenant-Governor cover the whole scope of the community's activities. His Honour George Bulyea was present for the official arrival in Edmonton of the Canadian Northern Railway of Mackenzie and Mann. Apparently, in the presence of thousands of Edmontonians and other visitors, His Honour "drove home with unerring blow the silver spike which held in place the first rail of the Canadian Northern Railway to reach the station in Edmonton."[95] His Honour John Bowen laid the cornerstone of the new Rutherford Library at the University of Alberta in the post-Second World War period.[96]

The personal and living bond between the Crown and ordinary people may become partially institutionalized through regular annual events such as The Canadian Derby, Consular Ball, Skating Parties or Garden Parties. Some functions such as the "Debutante's Balls" have fallen into disfavour. Albertans never fully accepted the viewpoint of Her Royal Highness Princess Margaret who suggested that these "coming-out into society rituals" ended in Britain because "Every tart in London was being presented."[97] As in Britain, they were abandoned in Alberta during the decade of the sixties. Other, similar

(City of Edmonton Archives, EA160-283)

### Debutantes Ball
A debutante presented to the Honourable John Bowlen and Mrs. Caroline Bowlen at the annual Debutantes Ball, 1954

presentations like the "Strauss Ball" have replaced this elegant social event. Likewise, "teas" have been replaced by other mixed receptions.

The Lieutenant-Governor also grants Vice-regal patronage to numerous organizations within the Alberta community which the holder of the office wishes to encourage. These societies range from the Edmonton Opera, Symphony and the Alberta Ballet, to various community-based clubs and organizations throughout the province. Two of the most established annual functions which the Lieutenant-Governor normally attends are the Canadian Derby and Consular Ball.

*The Canadian Derby*

The Canadian Derby began as a race in Winnipeg in 1929. By 1952 it had become apparent to racing fans that it lacked colour and excitement and Winnipeg fans were treating it as "just another horse race."[98] Consequently, in 1958 the Derby was moved to Edmonton. In 1960, the Edmonton Exhibition Association sought and received official patronage of the Derby from the Governor General of Canada. Thus, the greatest horse race in the West became officially "The Governor General's Canadian Derby." In addition, the Derby received its first permanent trophy when a commission to famed Alberta Sculptor, Charles Biel, produced a beautiful work of art for future classics. These changes allowed His Honour Percy Page to present the newly fashioned Governor General's trophy to the winning owners for the first time in 1960.[99] Finally, under the leadership of local sportsman, Walter H. Sprague, new ideas appeared in connection with the race. A Derby breakfast was begun which attracted most of the province's leading citizens. Colour was added to the racetrack with grandstand and infield decorations of daises. Alberta's Lieutenant-Governor was brought to the winner's enclosure by landau drawn by a team of hackneys and with a mounted escort of the Sheriff's Posse for the regal presentation ceremony to the winning owner.[100] In 1966, Jim Coleman noted that the Lieutenant-Governor, the Honourable Grant MacEwan, arrived in an open carriage and was escorted by "members of The Edmonton Posse.

The members of the possee were handsomely mounted but, in their flat black sombreros and their formal black suits, they resembled professional pallbearers, escorting a gun-slinger's corpse to the Boot Hill burial grounds."[101] In 1974, a driving rain assailed the track just before the Lieutenant-Governor arrived. When the deluge descended, the musicians ran for cover but not before water had entered some of their instruments. "When the trombonist essayed a glissando, he blew an arching plume of water 20 feet across the stage."[102] Edmonton still hosts this major race and the Lieutenant-Governors are generally in attendance, bringing pomp and colour to a fashionable and financially rewarding event.

*Consular Ball*

Another function at which the Lieutenant-Governor participates is the annual posh black-tie Consular Ball which began in 1980 when the province turned 75 and oil made Edmonton the capital of the "blue-eyed sheikdom". Because Alberta mattered, a half dozen full-time consuls opened diplomatic posts in the city. With the rise of Calgary to prominence and the weakness of the oil and gas industry in the intervening years, one by one these consulates closed their doors in the capital, leaving only the Japanese and Italian consulates as reminders of headier days. The Japanese Consul is now scheduled to leave Edmonton for Calgary also. Nevertheless, the Consular Ball has survived because of the presence of twenty-four Honourary Consuls who are either nationals of the country they serve or have professional ties there.

The evening begins with the walking in of the flags and the arrival of the

Royal Canadian Mounted Police and the Loyal Edmonton Regiment officers. With the entrance of the Vice-regal party, the Royal Anthem and National Anthem are played and the official welcome is given. Her Honour is seated next to the senior full-time diplomat in the room, the Japanese consul. The five-course meal is then served. Following dessert, the Japanese consul reminds those present of the university scholarship endowment and the Lieutenant-Governor is expected to make an appropriate speech for the occasion. The evening proceeds with the live band moving guests from dinner to the dance floor.[103] Because money is raised for the worthy cause of education, Lieutenant-Governors have been very supportive of this special annual social evening.

*Lieutenant-Governor Trophy ( The Bulyea Cup)*

One of the oldest events to which Alberta's Lieutenant-Governors are associated is the annual Music Festival. Originating in England, competitive Music Festivals began in Canada, in Edmonton, in May 1908. These festivals quickly spread to the other western provinces the following year and then on to the remainder of Canada after the First World War.

The initiative for the festival in Alberta came from His Honour George Bulyea who acted on a suggestion from the Governor General, Earl Grey. On the occasion of the ceremonies marking Alberta's entry into Confederation as a province in September 1905, the Governor General was impressed with the choral work performed and promoted the idea of bringing a number of choral groups together in Ottawa. Although invited, Alberta was unable to send any choirs to the nation's capital, but the notion spawned the idea of a competitive music festival for the province.

The first festival drew over one hundred entries in eleven classes of competition. The climax to this very successful event was a giant concert the final evening of the festival. It was organized by two musicians in the city, Vernon Barford, organist, choirmaster and conductor of the All Saints Anglican Cathedral Choir, and Howard Stutchbury, baritone and choirmaster. Before an audience of about two thousand at the Thistle Rink, a combined chorus of two hundred singers and forty instrumentalists performed.[104] The Lieutenant-Governor entered, the orchestra played the Royal Anthem and the concert began. Following the musical presentations, His Honour presented the prizes and shields.[105] Each year the Lieutenant-Governor, acting as a patron of the Alberta Music Festival, attended the final evening of the event to present the prizes and shields to the winners in each category.[106] In 1911, His Honour George Bulyea donated a cup "for the most artistic performance in any of the various competitions."[107] Ironically, that year the Lieutenant-Governor was unable to attend the final festival concert and Her Honour Annie Bulyea presented the Bulyea Cup to the All Saints Anglican Cathedral Choir.[108] Since those early years this festival has grown in size and the Bulyea Cup has been re-designated the "Lieutenant Governor Trophy" (1981) and awarded to the winner of the Senior Choir class at the festival. The Vice-regal representative in Alberta promoted such a worthy cause to help raise the standard of excellence in music throughout the province. This initiative has also aided Edmonton in becoming a musical centre of importance in Canada with the tradition continuing to this very day.

(Courtesy of First Presbyterian Church, Edmonton)

*Bulyea Cup*
The Bulyea Cup donated by the first Lieutenant-Governor of Alberta, the Honourable George Bulyea, to the Alberta Music Festival in 1911

231

## Bulyea Cup Winners

(City of Edmonton Archives, EA-346-10)

All Saints Anglican Choir, proud winners of the Bulyea Cup, 1911

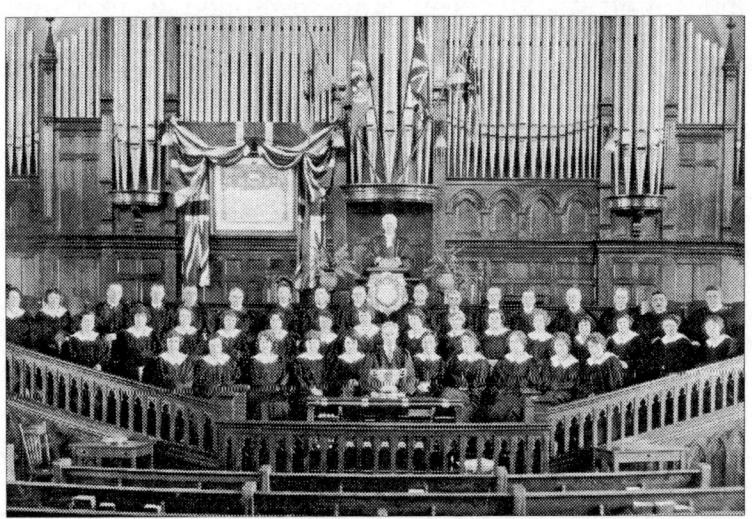

(Courtesy of First Presbyterian Church, Edmonton)

First Presbyterian Church Choir, proud winners of the Bulyea Cup, 1923

Other Occasions

On numerous occasions, the Lieutenant-Governor is often called upon to open various buildings and to unveil plaques and sculptures designed to make our environment more pleasant. Most often these ceremonies are very happy and spark enthusiastic praise by citizens. One such "unveiling" by Lieutenant-Governor Bowlen produced the opposite. At the end of May 1957, His Honour pressed a button to start the water flowing through the one and a half ton bronze fountain in front of Edmonton's new city hall building.[109] This bronze and water sculpture entitled "Migrants" consisted of an interpretation of nine Canada geese, four in flight and five standing, erected to symbolize Edmonton "as the aviation gateway to the north" and her pretensions to be "Canada's city of progress."[110] From the moment the Lieutenant-Governor turned on this fountain, conceived and fashioned by a Canadian, Lionel Thomas, criticism filled the "letters to the editor" page of the *Edmonton Journal*. All judgement focused on the "spaghetti tree"; fortunately, none was directed towards the Lieutenant-Governor who was attempting to connect with the community by promoting Canadian art in the broadest sense.

Letters poured into the *Edmonton Journal* attempting to find meaning in this "plumber's nightmare" and questioning whether geese really existed in this "rubbish". "No-can-see" claimed that "the scene presented looked less like a goose or geese than did the one we had for 'New Year' after we had eaten on it for three days."[111] "Concerned" called those "nine things...in the spray...a farce."[112] On opening day, Joan Doakes turned her puzzlement into a game "to find all the 'geese' in that mangled 'mess'." When walking away after the

*"Migrants"*

The bronze and water sculpture symbolizing Edmonton "as the aviation gateway to the North" and as "Canada's city of progress" was quickly dubbed the "Spaghetti Tree" by unappreciative Edmontonians of avant-garde art following His Honour John Bowlen's unveiling of the sculpture in May 1957. Today it stands neglected and rusting on the west side of the present City Hall

ceremony she looked back over her shoulder to see if distance aided the eye. Apparently, "It didn't."[113] Although many saw this contribution to Canadian art as "a plumber's mess", others saw it as a "study in nuclear fission" and still others a "a monument to spaghetti!" Some individuals like Edith Mills called for scraping the "twisted mass of pipes" in order to give Edmontonians something to "be proud of."[114] The wise city council ignored the voice of the people and their cost-conscious carping and kept the "eyesore", a monument to "the growth of indigenous Canadian art" as one wag remarked. It is unclear whether the unveiling by the Lieutenant-Governor preserved this "gaggle of geese"[115] from destruction when the 1957 City Hall gave way to the modern structure of the late 1980s. At any rate, this noble symbol of the city of Edmonton stands rusting and springing leaks in the piping in a nook on the west side of the present City Hall, a mere shadow of its splendour when unveiled by His Honour John Bowlen almost a half century ago!

Sometimes the Lieutenant-Governor is called upon to perform unexpected duties at various functions held for most worthy purposes. On the first week-end in October 1999, His Honour "Bud" Olson and Mrs. Olson travelled to Lac la Biche to help the town celebrate the 200th anniversary of David Thompson's arrival on the shores of Lac la Biche and the successful 135 km trek for a unit of the Royal Army (Territorial) Adventure Training exercise which ended at Lac la Biche. On that October week-end, the McGrane Branch of The Royal Canadian Legion led celebrations for both events. After His Honour reviewed a military parade, over 500 people gathered at a regimental style dinner. The head table, centred by His Honour and Mrs. Olson, spread out several metres on either side of them with numerous high-ranking military officers, politicians, First Nations' Chiefs and even the Military Advisor and Head of the British Defence Liaison Staff at the British High Commission in Ottawa.[116] With only one microphone and all the dignitaries wanting to speak, complications arose as speakers from various ends of the long head table vied for the microphone. To resolve a difficult situation, the Lieutenant-Governor agreed to hold the microphone and pass it along to the appropriate official on his left or right at the proper time for speech-making. As one close observer in

(Courtesy of Rod Stewart, Royal Canadian Legion, Alberta-N.W.T. Command)

### Lac la Biche Celebrations 1999
The banquet celebrating the arrival of David Thompson at Lac la Biche at which His Honour Bud Olson served as the unofficial "microphone passer" between each end of the head table.

the audience noted during the addresses, "Only The Royal Canadian Legion could get away with using the Lieutenant-Governor as a microphone stand."

Besides such impromptu service, the Lieutenant-Governors have participated in many other carefully considered undertakings. They have encouraged the pursuit of knowledge through formal educational and other activities such as Boy Scout and Girl Guides organizations. From the early days when young people were welcomed to Government House for parties, to the visits to schools made by more recent holders of the Vice-regal office,

Lieutenant-Governors have always focused on the young people of Alberta, the province's future. In all these ways, the Lieutenant-Governors are living examples of our traditions and highest ideals and unite the past, present and future of our community together.

Lieutenant-Governor Visits Schools

(Ed Kaiser, *The Edmonton Journal*)

His Honour Bud Olson talks to the grade 6 class about the Canadian Crown at Robert Rundle Elementary School at St. Albert, 5 December 1996

(Christine Vanzella, *Edmonton Sun*)

Lieutenant-Governor Bud Olson presents a portrait of Queen Elizabeth and Prince Phillip to Shanelle Murray at Robert Rundle Elementary School at St. Albert, 5 December 1996

Lieutenant-Governor Attends Banquets

(Courtesy of LT Col Frank Kozar, Edmonton)

Escorted by Robert Dunn, Her Honour Lois Hole attends the Right Honourable Sir Winston Churchill Banquet 23 May 2002

## Lieutenant-Governor Opens New Facilities

(Courtesy of April Bartlett, *St. Albert Gazette*)

Lieutenant-Governor Lois Hole opens a new Royal Canadian Mounted Police building at St. Albert

## NOTES

1. Francis Parkman, *France and England in North America: Jesuits in North America in the Seventeenth Century,* Boston: Little, Brown and Company, 1894, 334-335.

2. *Edmonton Journal,* 2 January 1907.

3. *Edmonton Bulletin,* 2 January 1908.

4. *Edmonton Bulletin,* 2 January 1909.

5. *Edmonton Bulletin,* 3 January 1911.

6. *Edmonton Journal,* 2 January 1913.

7. *Edmonton Bulletin,* 3 January 1928; *Edmonton Journal,* 2 January 1930.

8. *Edmonton Journal,* 2 January 1932.

9. *Edmonton Journal,* 2 January 1935.

10. *Edmonton Journal,* 2 January 1936.

11. *Edmonton Journal,* 2 January 1937.

12. *Edmonton Journal,* 3 January 1938.

13. *Edmonton Journal,* 2 January 1952.

14. *Edmonton Journal,* 3 January 1939.

15. *Edmonton Journal,* 2 January 1940.

16. *Edmonton Bulletin,* 2 January 1943.

17. *Edmonton Journal,* 2 January 1946.

18. *Edmonton Journal,* 3 January 1950.

19. A. W. (Tony) Cashman, *The Vice-Regal Cowboy: Life and Times of Alberta's J. J. Bowlen,* Edmonton: The Institute of Applied Art, Ltd., 1957, 191.

20. *Edmonton Journal,* 2 January 1953; 2 January 1954.

21. *Edmonton Journal,* 2 January 1953.

22. *Edmonton Journal*, 2 January 1957.

23. *Edmonton Journal*, 2 January 1960.

24. *Edmonton Journal*, 2 January 1964.

25. *Edmonton Journal*, 2 January 1965.

26. *Ibid.*

27. *Edmonton Journal*, 3 January 1966.

28. *Edmonton Journal*, 3 January 1967.

29. *Edmonton Journal*, 2 January 1975.

30. *Edmonton Journal*, 2 January 1976.

31. *Edmonton Journal*, 3 January 1978.

32. *Edmonton Sun*, 2 January 1981.

33. *Edmonton Journal*, 2 January 1985.

34. *Edmonton Journal*, 2 January 1987.

35. *Edmonton Journal*, 2 January 1996.

36. *Edmonton Sun*, 30 November 1996.

37. *Ibid.*

38. *Edmonton Sun*, 5 December 1996.

39. *Edmonton Journal*, 2 January 1997.

40. *Alberta Report*, 16 December 1996.

41. *Ibid.*

42. *Edmonton Sun*, 6 December 1996.

43. *Alberta Report*, 16 December 1996.

44. *Edmonton Journal*, 6 December 1996.

45. *Edmonton Sun*, 6 December 1996.

46. *Edmonton Journal*, 5 December 1996.

47. *Edmonton Sun*, 7 December 1996.

48. *Edmonton Journal*, 2 January 1997 & *Edmonton Sun*, 2 January 1997.

49. *Edmonton Journal*, 2 January 2001.

50. *Edmonton Journal*, 17 November 2000.

51. *Edmonton Journal*, 17 November 2000.

52. *Edmonton Journal*, 2 January 2001, B1.

53. *The Canada Gazette*, Tuesday 3 February 1957.

54. *Edmonton Journal*, 22 May 2001, B1.

55. Robert Cupido, 'Appropriating the Past: Pageants, Politics, and the Diamond Jubilee of Confederation" in *Journal of the Canadian Historical Association*, 1998, 158.

56. *Edmonton Journal*, 2 July 2002, B1 & 3.

57. *Edmonton Bulletin*, 11 November 1926.

58. David Cannadine, "War and Death, Grief and Mourning in Modern Britain" in Joachim Shaley, ed. *Mirrors of Mortality: Studies in the Social History of Death,* New York: St. Martin's Press, [1981], 218.

59. *Ibid.*, 219.

60. *Ibid.*, 219-220.

61. *Ibid.*, 226.

62. *Edmonton Journal*, 11 November 1919.

63. *Edmonton Journal*, 11 November 1920.

64. *Edmonton Journal*, 13 November 1923.

65. Clifford H. Bowering, *Service: The Story of the Canadian Legion 1925-1960*, Ottawa: Dominion Command, Canadian Legion, [1960], 200-201.

66. Bowering, *Service,* 202-203.

67. *Edmonton Bulletin,* 11 November 1922.

68. *Edmonton Senior,* November 2000, 7.

69. *Legion Magazine,* 74.1 (January/February 1999), 2 "Alberta-N.W.T. Command, The Royal Canadian Legion".

70. *Legion Magazine,* 75.1 (January/February 2000), 13 "Alberta-N.W.T. Command, The Royal Canadian Legion"; 76.1 (January/February 2001), 5 "Alberta-N.W.T. Command, The Royal Canadian Legion".

71. *Edmonton Bulletin,* 12 November 1924.

72. *Edmonton Journal,* 11 November 1925.

73. *Edmonton Bulletin,* 11 November 1926.

74. *Edmonton Bulletin,* 11 November 1927.

75. *Edmonton Bulletin,* 11 November 1927.

76. *Edmonton Bulletin,* 15 April 1936. City of Edmonton Archives, *Cenotaph File.*

77. *Edmonton Journal,* 10 November 1936.

78. Denise C. Thomson, *National Sorrow, National Pride: Canada and the Memory of the Great War, 1918-1945,* M. A. History degree, University of Alberta, 1995, 53-57.

79. *Edmonton Bulletin,* 9 November 1942.

80. *Edmonton Journal,* 12 November 1953.

81. *Edmonton Journal,* 11 November 1970; 12 November 1970; 12 November 1977.

82. *Edmonton Sun,* 12 November 1978.

83. *Edmonton Sun,* 12 November 1984; 12 November 1985; 12 November 1986.

84. *Edmonton Sun,* 12 November 1987.

85. *Edmonton Sun,* 11 November 1988.

86. *Ibid.*

87.*Edmonton Sun,* Sunday, 11 November 1990, 5.

88.*Edmonton Journal,* 12 November 1990.

89.*Edmonton Sun,* Sunday 11 November 1990, 5.

90.*Alberta Report,* 16 December 1996, 16.

91.http://www.gov.ab.ca/acn/200010/9813.html (*Government of Alberta News Release, The Alberta Order of Excellence,* Edmonton, 17 October 2000.

92.*Edmonton Journal,* 3 January 2002, A6.

93.http://www.theaward.org,

94.Jacques Monet, *The Canadian Crown,* Toronto: Clarke, Irwin & Company, [1979], 75-77.

95.James G. MacGregor, *A History of Alberta,* Edmonton: Hurtig Publsihers, [1972], 191.

96.John Macdonald, *The History of the University of Alberta 1908-1958,* Toronto: W.J. Gage, for the University of Alberta, 1968, 77.

97.*National Post,* Monday 11 February 2002, A10.

98.Morris Taylor, *Canadian Derby History,*

99.*Edmonton Journal,* Monday, 12 August 1960, 13.

100.*Edmonton Journal,* Monday, 21 August 1961, Section 1, p.6 & Section 2, p. 13.

101.*Edmonton Journal,* Monday 22 August 1966.

102.*Edmonton Journal,* Monday 26 August 1974.

103.*Edmonton Journal,* 28 May 2001, B1.

104.Helmut Kallmann, *A History of Music in Canada 1534-1914,* [Toronto]: University of Toronto Press, [1960], 218-219.

105.*Edmonton Bulletin,* Wednesday 6 May 1908, 1.

106.*Edmonton Bulletin,* Thursday 6 May 1909, 1&6; Friday 6 May 1910,3.

107.*Edmonton Bulletin,* Monday 15 May 1911, 1 & 8.

108. *Edmonton Bulletin,* Friday 19 May 1911, 9; Edmonton *Journal,* Friday 19 May 1911.

109. *Edmonton Journal,* Friday 31 May 1957, 1; Saturday 1 June 1957, 4.

110. These quotations are taken from the plaque on the fountain.

111. *Edmonton Journal,* Tuesday 4 June 1957, 4.

112. *Edmonton Journal,* Wednesday 5 June 1957, 6.

113. *Edmonton Journal,* Saturday 8 June 1957, 4.

114. *Edmonton Journal,* Wednesday 5 June 1957, 6.

115. *Edmonton Journal,* Monday 10 June 1957.

116. Legion Magazine, 74.1 (January/February 1999), *Alberta-N.W.T. Command, The Royal Canadian Legion,* 10.

# VI

## CONCLUSION

The constitutional monarchy and the Maple Crown are integral parts of Canada's history. Since contact between the European powers and the First Nations, the social and cultural fabric of the country and its political institutions have found expression through the Crown. The Office of Governor General and Lieutenant-Governor have existed since the French regime and have continued without interruption through the British era and into the modern Canadian period. Undoubtedly, the success of the constitutional monarchy has been its flexibility and adaptability to change over time. The three-fold nature of the Maple Crown has enabled it to serve Canada's multi-cultural citizenry well in a country organized within a federal system of government. With the Sovereign embodying all Canadians and symbolizing our hopes and aspirations as a people, the Crown is key to the identity and sovereignty of Canada.

In the past 100 years, the Office of Lieutenant-Governor has emerged from under the shadow of the Office of Governor General. While originally Lieutenant-Governors were officers of the federal government, they have come into the daylight to exercise sovereignty within the provincial sphere of jurisdiction in the same manner the Governors General play that role at the federal level in Canada. Alberta's Lieutenant-Governors have been instrumental in this changed role as witnessed by the active role His Honour John Bowen took in protecting the constitution against improper action taken by Premier Aberhart. In the more symbolic realm, His Honour John Bowlen raised the status of the Lieutenant-Governors by visiting the Queen at her official residence in Britain in the same way Governors General did. This change in status of Lieutenant-Governors has also been hampered in Alberta by unwise elected officials who have closed or demolished the official residence of the Crown's representative, who have reduced the Vice-regal staff to a minimum or who have diminished ceremonial occasions which could enhance the position and place of the Vice-regal personages within the community. Some of these failures have been mitigated through the Governor General's Office in granting unique flags or "standards" and "badges" to all Lieutenant-Governors. Many elected officials have failed to realize the importance of ritual in the life of ordinary Canadians living in Alberta.

Through the ceremony, pageantry and colour associated with the Crown, Canadians are inspired to look beyond our own needs and comforts to embrace the sense of wonder and grandeur of life which is greater than the ordinary day-to-day too-busy schedules people keep. These very rituals have come into being to help us to differentiate the mundane from the special. The Canadian Crown helps us to remember that there are times in life when it is important to pay homage and respect. The Office of Lieutenant-Governor in Alberta plays a vital role in the presence and functioning of this Maple Crown in Canada and thus reminding us, from time to time, that worshiping convenience above all else reduces our humanity and prevents us from reaching beyond the usual to attain our dreams.

God save The Queen!

(Larry Wong, The Edmonton Journal)

### The Crown Embraces All Canadians

The Maple Crown, through the Monarch, Governor General and Lieutenant-Governors, protects the rights of Canadians, consoles their sorrows and celebrates their joys and achievements. At the Canada Day festivities, 1 July 2002, Her Honour Lois Hole, Lieutenant-Governor of Alberta, with one of her traditional Vice-regal hugs, shares the excitement of 8 year old Rita Baumann who moments before became a Canadian citizen at the Citizenship Ceremony on the Legislature Grounds of Alberta

# VII

# POSTSCRIPT

On the evening of Thursday, 6 January 2005, the Lieutenant-Governor's Standard was lowered above the front entrance to the Legislature Building, signalling that Her Honour Lois Hole had died at the Royal Alexandra Hospital in Edmonton from peritoneal (abdominal) cancer. Her Honour's last public appearance had occurred on 16 November 2004 when she participated in the public announcement that a new women's hospital at the Royal Alexandra Hospital would be named "The Lois Hole Hospital for Women". With Premier Klein in attendance, she again approached the political sphere by suggesting that the new hospital "is a sign that Albertans remain committed to public health care."[1] As she was helped into her wheelchair and the end of the ceremony by her senior aide-de-camp, Captain George Kuhse, she thanked everyone for the special afternoon and said that "If I had the time, I'd give you all a hug right now...."[2] With those words, "the queen of hugs" passed from public appearance for the last time.

In place of a state funeral, the family of the late Lieutenant-Governor opted for a public memorial service which was held in Edmonton on 18 January 2005 at the Winspear Centre with overflow venues elsewhere. Controversy surrounded this occasion because of the absence of the Governor General of Canada, Her Excellency Adrienne Clarkson. Many Albertans blamed Her Excellency for this *faux pas* in a time of provincial grieving,[3] rather than the political advisors of Adrienne Clarkson who had asked Her Excellency to represent Canada at the inauguration of Ukraine's new president, Viktor Yushchenko.[4] Echoing the disappointment expressed by Premier Ralph Klein of Alberta, Dan MacLennan, president of the Alberta Union of Provincial Employees is probably correct when he stated that most Albertans will view the Governor General's absence as "unforgivable, beyond reason and unjustifiable."[5] By not attending the Memorial Service for Her Honour Lois Hole because she had to accept the advice of her Prime Minister under our constitutional system of government, her Excellency Adrienne Clarkson has undoubtedly left an undeserved stain on an otherwise exemplary tenure of office through no fault of her own.[6] Her Excellency's political advisors simply misunderstood the depth and strength of the feelings of the people of Alberta at the death of The Honourable Lois Hole.

At the time of Her Honour Lois Hole's death, the government of Alberta came to a standstill. Because the Administrator is attached to the person and not the office of Lieutenant-Governor, when Her Honour died, the Chief Justice of Alberta, Catherine Fraser, ceased to be able to assume the role of Administrator. No appointments could be made, no legislation could be proclaimed, and no date could be officially set for the opening of the new Session of the Legislature until a new Lieutenant-Governor was appointed. Finally, on Thursday, 20 January 2005, the Lieutenant-Governor's standard was raised above the Legislature Building's main entrance, informing the public that a new Lieutenant-Governor, His Honour Norman Kwong, had been installed at Government House in Edmonton as the sixteenth Lieutenant-Governor of Alberta.

In a brief ceremony before his wife and a number of dignitaries, His Honour Norman Kwong took the oath of office which was administered by Chief Justice Catherine Fraser.  In a moving speech at his installation, His Honour spoke about how his immigrant father could not vote until his 40th year in Canada, and yet his son was now Lieutenant-Governor of Alberta.  He was proud to point out that there are "not many places where you can achieve that kind of success."[7]

In his installation speech, His Honour Norman Kwong said he would do his best to serve all Albertans and "would like to use his new position to promote wellness and physical activity among Alberta's youth."[8]  This goal led to controversy when His Honour said he favoured a province-wide workplace smoking ban in order to promote healthy living and well-being in the province in opposition to Premier Ralph Klein's opposition to the suggestion.[9]  His Honour learned early how difficult it will be to be less outspoken than former Lieutenant-Governor Lois Hole about proposed government policy.

Albertans were delighted that Governor General Adrienne Clarkson had appointed Norman Kwong as Lieutenant-Governor.  Born in Calgary, His Honour played football for both the Calgary Stampeders and Edmonton Eskimos football clubs and won four Grey Cups; as part owner of the Calgary Flames hockey team, he also won a Stanley Cup.  Named a Member of the Order of Canada in 1988, Kwong has contributed to the province in the sporting, cultural and business world.[10]  He is well suited to take up his new official duties as Lieutenant-Governor.  Unfortunately, because the province demolished the official residence of the Lieutenant-Governor in 2004, it was unclear at the time of his installation where he would reside officially as he undertakes this challenging position as Her Majesty's Alberta representative during this important year in Alberta's history.

During 2005, the spotlight will shine on The Honourable Norman Kwong as Alberta celebrates its centennial as a province of Canada. His Honour will not only welcome the Queen and Prince Philip, but he will also partake in countless other celebratory events throughout the province. Albertans sensed that the installation of His Honour Norman Kwong marked an auspicious beginning to their year-long festivities.

*Installation Ceremony*
His Honour Norman Kwong at Government House.
Thursday, 20 January 2005

(Courtesy of Larry Wong, *Edmonton Journal*)

## NOTES

1. *Edmonton Journal,* Wednesday, 17 November 2004, A1.

2. *Edmonton Journal,* Wednesday, 17 November 2004, A14.

3. *Edmonton Journal,* Wednesday, 19 January 2005, A12. (See "Letters" under the heading "Clarkson is wasting time in Ukraine".

4. *Edmonton Sun,* Wednesday, 19 January 2005, 5.; *Edmonton Journal,* Sunday, 23 January 2005, A5; *Globe and Mail,* Saturday, 22 January 2005, A6.

5. *Edmonton Sun,* Wednesday, 19 January 2005, 5.

6. *Globe and Mail,* Saturday, 22 January 2005, A6.

7. *Edmonton Journal,* Friday, 21 January 2005, A6.

8. *Edmonton Sun,* Friday, 21 January 2005, 16.

9. *Edmonton Journal,* Friday, 21 January 2005, A6.

10. *Edmonton Journal,* Thursday, 20 January 2005, A17.

# APPENDICES
## A
### Installation

| | |
|---|---|
| The Honourable George H. V. Bulyea | 01 September 1905 |
| The Honourable Dr. Robert G. Brett | 20 October 1915 |
| The Honourable Dr. William Egbert | 29 October 1925 |
| The Honourable William L. Walsh | 05 May 1931 |
| The Honourable Colonel Philip C. H. Primrose | 01 October 1936 |
| The Honourable John C. Bowen | 23 March 1937 |
| The Honourable John J. Bowlen | 01 February 1950 |
| The Honourable J. Percy Page | 19 December 1959 |
| The Honourable J. W. Grant MacEwan | 6 January 1966 |
| The Honourable Ralph G. Steinhauer | 2 July 1974 |
| The Honourable Frank Lynch-Staunton | 18 October 1979 |
| The Honourable W. Helen Hunley | 22 January 1985 |
| The Honourable T. Gordon Towers | 11 March 1991 |
| The Honourable H. A. "Bud" Olson | 17 April 1996 |
| The Honourable Lois Hole | 10 February 2000 |
| The Honourable Norman Kwong | 20 January 2005 |

B

## Visit With The Queen

| | |
|---|---|
| His Honour, the Honourable John Bowlen<br>(First visit by a Lieutenant-Governor) | Thursday, 28 June 1956 |
| His Honour, the Honourable Percy Page | *no visit* |
| His Honour, the Honourable Grant MacEwan | *no visit* |
| His Honour, the Honourable Ralph Steinhauer<br>(Buckingham Palace) | 30 June 1976 |
| His Honour, the Honourable Frank Lynch-Staunton<br>(Windsor Castle luncheon) | 13 April 1983 |
| Her Honour, the Honourable Helen Hunley<br>(Buckingham Palace) | Tuesday, 26 July 1988 |
| His Honour, the Honourable Gordon Towers<br>(Buckingham Palace) | Tuesday, 13 October 1992 |
| His Honour, the Honourable H. A. "Bud" Olson | *no visit* |
| Her Honour, the Honourable Lois Hole<br>(Buckingham Palace) | 01 November 2000 |

## C

## Honourary Degrees from the University of Alberta

| | | |
|---|---|---|
| His Honour, the Honourable George Bulyea | LLD | 1908 |
| His Honour, the Honourable Robert Brett | LLD | 1915 |
| His Honour, the Honourable William Egbert | LLD | 1927 |
| His Honour, the Honourable William Walsh | LLD | 1932 |
| His Honour, the Honourable Colonel Philip Primrose | *no honourary degree awarded* | |
| His Honour, the Honourable John Bowen | LLD | 1939 |
| His Honour, the Honourable John Bowlen | LLD | 1952 |
| His Honour, the Honourable Percy Page | LLD | 1961 |
| His Honour, the Honourable Grant MacEwan | LLD | 1966 |
| His Honour, the Honourable Ralph Steinhauer | LLD | 1976 |
| His Honour, the Honourable Frank Lynch-Staunton | LLD | 1980 |
| Her Honour, the Honourable Helen Hunley | LLD | 1985 |
| His Honour, the Honourable Gordon Towers | LLD | 1992 |
| His Honour, the Honourable H. A. "Bud" Olson | LLD | 1996 |
| Her Honour, the Honourable Lois Hole | LLD | 2000 |

## D

### Most Venerable Order of the Hospital of St. John of Jerusalem

| | |
|---|---|
| His Honour George H. V. Bulyea | *not invested* |
| His Honour Dr. Robert G. Brett | *not invested* |
| His Honour Dr. William Egbert | *not invested* |
| His Honour William Walsh | *not invested* |
| His Honour Philip Primrose | *not invested* |
| His Honour John Bowen | 17 September 1949 (Alberta) |
| His Honour John Bowlen | 23 November 1953 (Alberta) |
| His Honour Percy Page | 30 October 1964 (Ottawa) |
| His Honour Grant MacEwan | *not invested* |
| His Honour Ralph Steinhauer | 29 September 1975 (Alberta) |
| His Honour Frank Lynch-Staunton | 24 October 1980 (Ottawa) |
| Her Honour Helen Hunley (Dame of Grace) | 18 October 1985 (Ottawa) |
| His Honour Gordon Towers (Knight of Grace) | 23 May 1991,(Alberta) |
| His Honour "Bud" Olson (Knight of Grace) | 31 May 1996 (Alberta) |
| Her Honour Lois Hole | 9 June 2000 (Dame of Justice) |

E

## Portrait Unveiling

His Honour George H. V. Bulyea

His Honour Dr. Robert G. Brett

His Honour Dr. William Egbert

His Honour William L. Walsh　　　　　Monday, 7 January 1974

His Honour Colonel Philip C.H. Primrose

His Honour John C. Bowen　　　　　Wednesday, 22 October 1975

His Honour John J. Bowlen

His Honour J. Percy Page　　　　　Wednesday, 29 October 1975

His Honour J. W. Grant MacEwan

His Honour Ralph G. Steinhauer　　　　　Friday, 29 April 1983

His Honour Frank C. Lynch-Staunton　　　　　Thursday, 3 September 1987

Her Honour W. Helen Hunley　　　　　Friday, 26 April 1991

His Honour T. Gordon Towers　　　　　Monday, 17 June 1996

His Honour H. A. "Bud" Olson　　　　　Thursday, 23 November 2000

## F

### Deaths and State Funerals

| | |
|---|---|
| His Honour George Bulyea | 28 July 1928 (Peachland, BC) |
| His Honour Robert Brett | 16 September 1929 (Calgary) |
| His Honour William Egbert | 15 October 1936 (Calgary) |
| His Honour William Walsh | 13 January 1938 (Victoria, BC) |
| His Honour Philip Primrose | 17 March 1937 (Edmonton) –State Funeral |
| His Honour John Bowen | 2 January 1957 (Edmonton) |
| His Honour John Bowlen | 16 December 1959 (Edmonton) –State Funeral |
| His Honour Percy Page | 2 March 1973 (Edmonton) |
| His Honour Grant MacEwan | 15 June 2000 (Calgary) –State Funeral |
| His Honour Ralph Steinhauer | 19 September 1987 (Edmonton) |
| His Honour Frank Lynch-Staunton | 25 September 1990 (Edmonton) |
| Her Honour Helen Hunley | ---------------------------------------- |
| His Honour Gordon Towers | 8 June 1999 (Red Deer) |
| His Honour "Bud" Olson | 14 February 2002 (Medicine Hat) |
| Her Honour Lois Hole | 6 January 2005 (Edmonton) |
| His Honour Norman Kwong | ---------------------------------------- |

## G

### Royal Visits to Alberta Since 1951

1951 (October) — Her Royal Highness The Princess Elizabeth and His Royal Highness The Duke of Edinburgh
(Alberta as part of their across Canada tour)

1958 (July-August) — Her Royal Highness The Princess Margaret
(Banff and Calgary)

1959 (July) — Her Majesty The Queen and His Royal Highness The Duke of Edinburgh
(across Canada tour)

1963 (30 January) — Her Majesty The Queen and His Royal Highness The Duke of Edinburgh
(unscheduled fueling stop in Edmonton)

1964 (17 September) — Her Royal Highness Princess Patricia (Lady Patricia Ramsay)
(To celebrate the Jubilee of the Princess Patricia's Light Infantry Regiment)

1967 (May-June) — Her Royal Highness Princess Albexandra, The Honourable Lady Ogilvy and Angus Ogilvy
(Banff, Calgary and Edmonton)

1968 (3-8 July) — Their Royal Highnesses the Duke and Duchess of Kent
(To open the Calgary Stampede)

1973 (June-July) — Her Majesty The Queen and His Royal Highness The Duke of Edinburgh
(To participate in events marking the RCMP centennial)

1977 (5-9 July) — His Royal Highness The Prince of Wales & His Royal

Highness The Duke of York
(Celebrations of signing of Treaty 7 and the Calgary stampede)

1978 (26 July-12 August) Her Majesty The Queen, His Royal Highness The Duke of Edinburgh, His Royal Highness The Prince Andrew and His Royal Highness The Prince Edward
(The Commonwealth Games at Edmonton)

1979 (25 October) His Royal Highness The Duke of Edinburgh
(Calgary to attend meeting of the Commonwealth Study Conference)

1980 (19-22 May) His Royal Highness The Duke of Edinburgh
HRH The Duke of Edinburgh's Fifth Commonwealth Study Conference)

1980 (18-28 July) Her Royal Highness The Princess Margaret, Countess of Snowdon
(marking the 75$^{th}$ anniversary of Alberta's entry into Confederation)

1983 (June-1 July) His Royal Highness The Prince of Wales and Diana, The Princess of Wales
(Edmonton for the Official opening of the 1983 World Universities Games)

1985 (19-21 August) His Royal Highness The Duke of Edinburgh
(Banff, Centennial of Parks Canada; Duke of Edinburgh's Award; New banners to Royal Canadian Army Cadets; Lake Louise designation of World Heritage Site and Arrival and departure ceremonies at Calgary Airport)

(July) Her Majesty Queen Elizabeth The Queen Mother
(CFB Cold Lake unscheduled stop & Edmonton, 5$^{th}$ Angus Forum)

1986 (June) Her Royal Highness The Princess Royal (The Princess Anne)
(Calgary as President of the British Olympic Association)

1987 (July)           His Royal Highness The Duke of York and The Duchess of
                      York
                      (Edmonton, Medicine Hat stampede and Head-Smashed-In-
                      Buffalo Jump

1988 (12-22 February) Her Royal Highness The Princess Royal (The Princess Anne)
                      (Calgary attended the XVth Winter Olympic Games as
                      President of the British Olympic Association

1990 (27June-1July)Her Majesty The Queen
                      (Calgary, Red Deer)

1991 (October)        His Royal Highness The Prince Edward
                      (Calgary, Gold award presentations)

1992 (March)          His Royal Highness The Duke of Edinburgh
                      (Calgary and CFB Suffield, World Wildlife Federation)

(14-17 July)          His Royal Highness The Duke of Edinburgh
                      (Calgary for the Royal Agricultural Society of the
                      Commonwealth Conference)

(11-14 November)      His Royal Highness The Prince Michael of Kent
                      (Edmonton, Remembrance Day & Canadian Finals Rodeo,
                      Lake Louise & Calgary, regimental events)

1993 (27 March)       His Royal Highness The Prince Edward
                      (Edmonton, Duke of Edinburgh Awards presentation)

1994 (August)         His Royal Highness The Prince Edward
                      (Calgary, Duke of Edinburgh's Awards)

1997 (19-20March)     His Royal Highness The Duke of Edinburgh
                      (World Wildlife Federation press conference, presentation of
                      gold award certificates, The Duke of Edinburgh's Award)

2001(2-3 August)      Their Royal Highnesses The Earl and Countess of Wessex
                      (Edmonton, attended 8th IAAF World Championships in

Athletics and Gold Award Ceremony for the Duke of Edinburgh's Award)

2002 (17-18March)  His Royal Highness The Prince Michael of Kent (Edmonton, Her Majesty's Golden Jubilee Celebrations)

# BIBLIOGRAPHY

## NEWSPAPERS

*Edmonton Bulletin*
*Edmonton Journal*
*The National Post*
*Edmonton Sun*

## ARCHIVAL SOURCES

First Presbyterian Archives

King, Dorothy May. *Childhood Memories of Edmonton Alberta 1902-1911, 1977.*

City of Edmonton Archives

Remembrance Day File

Cenotaph File

Lieutenant-Governors Files

Frank Oliver File

Provincial Archives of Alberta

## GOVERNMENTAL AND INSTITUTIONAL DOCUMENTS

University of Alberta. *Calendar 2000/2001, no boundaries.*

## SECONDARY SOURCES

Books

Babcock, D.R. *A Gentleman of Strathcona: Alexander Cameron Rutherford*. [Calgary]: Univesity of Calgary Press and Friends of Rutherford House, [1989].

Barr, John J. *The Dynasty: The Rise and Fall of Social Credit in Alberta*. [Toronto]: McClelland and Stewart, [1974].

Blakeslee, Fred Gilbert. *Uniforms of the World*. New York: E.P. Dutton & Co., [1929].

Bousfield, Arthur and Garry Toffoli. *Royal Observations: Canadians & Royalty*. Toronto: Dundurn Press, 1991.

Bowering, Clifford H. *Service: The Story of the Canadian Legion 1925-1960*. Ottawa: Dominion Command, Canadian Legion, [1960].

Cashman, A.W. (Tony) *The Vice-Regal Cowboy*. Edmonton: The Institute of Applied Art., 1957.

Dolphin, Frank. *The Alberta Legislature: A Celebration,* Edmonton: Plains Publishing Ltd., 1987.

Elliott, David R. and Iris Miller, *Bible Bill: A Biography of William Aberhart,* [Edmonton]: Reidmore Books, [1987].

Evans, A. Margaret. *Sir Oliver Mowat,* Toronto: University of Toronto Press, [1992].

Farnell, Peggy O'Connor. *Old Glenora*. Edmonton: Old Glenora Historical Society, 1984.

Griesbach, W. A. *I Remember*. Toronto: Ryerson Press, [1946].

Hall, Trevor. *Royal Canada*. Godalming, Surrey, England: Archive Publishing,

[1989].

Hichens, Phoebe. *All About the Royal Family*. [London: Macmillan, 1981].

Hooke, Alfred J. *30+5 I Know, I was there*. [Edmonton]: [Insitute of Applied Art], [1971].

Hubbard, R.H. *Ample Mansions: The Viceregal Residences of the Canadian Provinces*. Ottawa: University of Ottawa Press, [1989].

Hugo, Victor. *The Hunchback of Notre Dame*. New York: [Random House], [1941].

Jackson, D. Michael. *The Canadian Monarchy in Saskatchewan*. 2$^{nd}$ edition. Regina: Government of Saskatchewan, 1990.

Johnson, L.P.V. and Ola J. MacNutt, *Aberhart of Alberta,* [Edmonton]: [Institute of Applied Art], [1070].

Kennedy, Fred. *Alberta was my Beat*. [Calgary]: The Albertan, 1975.

Léger, Jules. *Jules Léger, Gouverneur Général du Canada/Governor General of Canada 1974-1979*. [Montréal]: La Presse, [1982].

Lynch-Staunton, Frank. *Greener Pastures: The Memoris of F. Lynch-Staunton*. Edmonton: Jasper Printing Group, 1987.

Macdonald, R.H. *Grant MacEwan: No Ordinary Man,* Saskatoon: Western Producer Prairie Books, [1979].

MacDonnell, Tom. *Daylight Upon Magic: The Royal Tour of Canada—1939*. Toronto: Macmillan, [1989].

McDougall, D. Blake, John E. McDonough and Kenneth W. Tingley. *Lieutenant-Governors of the Northwest Territories and Alberta 1876-1991*. Edmonton: Alberta Legislature Library, 1991.

MacGregor, James G. *A History of Alberta*. Edmonton: Hurtig Publishers, [1972].

MacKinnon, Frank. *The Crown in Canada.* [Calgary]: Glenbow-Alberta Institute, McClelland and Stewart West, [1976].

Monet, Jacques, S.J. *The Canadian Crown.* Toronto: Clarke, Irwin & Company, [1979].

Morton, Desmond and Glenn Wright. *Winning the Second Battle: Canadian Veterans and the Return to Civilian Life 1915-1930.* Toronto: University of Toronto Press, [1987].

Mowat, Claire. *Pomp and Circumstances.* Toronto: Seal edition, McClelland-Bantam, [1992].

Saywell, John T. *The Office of Lieutenant-Governor: A Study in Canadian Government and Politics.* Toronto: University of Toronto Press, 1957.

*Silver Jubilee, Royal Visit to Canada, Six Days in the Life of the Queen.* Ottawa: Deneau & Greenberg, 1977.

Smith, David E. *The Invisible Crown: The First Principle of Canadian Government.* Toronto: University of Toronto Press, [1995].

_____. *The Republican Option in Canada, Past and Present.* Toronto: University of Toronto Press, [1999].

Stamp, Robert M. *Kings, Queens & Canadians: A celebration of Canada's infatuation with the British Royal Family.* [Markham, Ontario]: Fitzhenry & Whiteside, [1987].

Stursburg, Peter. *Roland Michener, The Last Viceroy,* Toronto: McGraw-Hill Ryerson, [1989].

*Sumbols of Canada.* [Ottawa]: Canadian Heritage, [1999].

Thomas, L.G. *The Liberal Party in Alberta: A History of Politics in the Province of Alberta 1905-1921,* Toronto: University of Toronto Press, 1959.

Von Hauff, Donna. *Everyone's Grandfather: The Life & Times of Grant MacEwan.* [Edmonton]: [Grant MacEwan Community College Foundation/Quon Editions], [1994].

Watkins, Ernest. *The Golden Province: A Political History of Alberta.* Calgary: Sandstone Publishing, [1980].

Yanish, Lori and Shirley Lowe. *Edmonton's West Side Story: The history of the original West End of Edmonton from 1870.* [ Edmonton: Jasper Printing Co., 1991].


Articles

Barnhart, Gordon. "The Queen in Saskatchewan" *Canadian Parliamentary Review,* 10.4 (Winter 1987-8), 14-15.

Blain, Douglas J. "Symbols of Sovereignty" *Canadian Parliamentary Review,* 4 (1981-82), 21-22.

Cannadine, David. "War and Death, Grief and Mourning in Modern Britain", in *Mirrors of Mortality: Studies in the Social History of Death,* ed. Joachim Whaley, New York: St. Martin's Press, [1981], 187-242.

Cupido, Robert. "Appropriating the Past: Pageants, Politics, and the Diamond Jubilee of Confederation", in *the Journal of the Canadian Historical Association 1998,* New Series, Vol. 9, 155-186.

Dacks, Barbara. "Her Honour Lois Hole, Alberta's New Lieutenant-Governor speaks her mind and follows her heart", *Legacy,* (fall 2000), 32.

Foran, Dr. Maxwell. "Excerpt from the euology to former Lieutenant-Governor Grant MacEwan", *Legacy,* (fall 2000), 3.

Garrison, Gary and Brian Hodgson, "Alberta's Black Rod: A gift of service and Commonwealth unity", *The Parliamentarian,* (April 1998), 199-200.

Hilliard, Harold. "He's a Vice-regal Cowboy", *Star Weekly,* 20 August 1955, 7.

Jackson, Michael, "How the monarchy protects Canadian values", *Canadian Speeches: Issues of the day.* 9.2 (May 1995), 40-47.

Saywell, John T. "The Lieutenant-Governors" in *The Provincial Political Systems, comparative essays,* eds. David J. Bellamy, Jon H. Pammett and Donald C. Rowat, Toronto: Metheun, [1976], 297-309.

_____. "Liberal Politics, Federal Policies, and the Lieutenant-Governor: Saskatchewan and Alberta 1905", *Saskatchewan History* 8(1955), 81-89.

Ward, Norman. "Hon. James Gardiner and the Liberal Party of Alberta, 1935-40", *Canadian Historical Review,* 51.3 (September 1975), 303-322.

Booklets

"Queen of Canada, 1952-1977", *Monarchy Canada.* 7.3 (September 1977), 1-64.


Theses

Thomson, Denise Carol. "National Sorrow, National Pride: Canada and the Memory of the Great War, 1918-1945", M.A. Thesis, Univesity of Alberta, 1995.

Waddell, William S. "The Honorable Frank Oliver", M.A. Thesis, Vols. I & II, University of Alberta, 1950.

# INDEX

Aberhart, William becomes Premier 96-97; closes Government House 61-63; relations with Bowen 100-102;112;113;158;159;160; 213
Administrator 14; 250
Alberta Order of Excellence 216-217
Alexander of Tunis, Viscount 27;79
Amerongen, Gerry 136
Angus, Constable Stewart 221
Athlone, Earl of 65
Alice, Princess 65

Barford, Vernon 229
Baumann, Rita 247
Bennett, R. B. 77; 125
Bessborough, Lord 26; 165
Black Rod 146-147
Bowen, Edith 53
Bowen, John 17;18;27; broadcasting Speech from the Throne, 155; conflict with Aberhart, 100-102; 158-159, 160; Government House closing 62-63; installation, 129-130; leaves Government House 66; licence plate difficulties 73; 100; New Years' Levee, 189; refuses ministerial advice 113; Remembrance Day, 213; thought of dismissing Aberhart 112; wears British Civil Dress Uniform 46; 224
Bowlen, John 17; bio. 130-132; built his own residence 67; 79; Debutantes' Ball, 225; installation, 130; Mount Bowlen, 130-131; New Years' Levee,189-190;receives honourary degree 81; Speech from the Throne, 150, 161, 162; State Funeral, 175-176; unveils "Migrants", 232-234; visit to sovereign 20; wears "Windsor" uniform 46;
Brett, Robert 26; bio. 122-123; installation 122; uses carriage as transportation 71; uses car as transportation 72;
Broonfield, Adrian 193
Brown, Harley 168
Brownlee, John 60; becomes Premier 95-96; resigns 96; 127
Bulyea Cup 228-231
Bulyea, George 25; 54; garden party at Government House 59; installation, 121-122; New Years' Levee, 188; Speech from the Throne, 148-149, 154;receives first honourary degree from the University of Alberta 82; selects fist Premier 94; stops Cushing from becoming Premier 95; 224
Bulyea, Annie 188
Byng, Lord 124

Cameron, Major D. F. 174
Canada Day 204-205;247
Canadian Derby 226-227
Carroll, Henry 16
Carter, David designs robe for Helen Hunley 48
Cashman, Tony 189
Chair special Chair from North West Territories Legislature used as throne, 135-137; gift from the City of Edmonton, 147-148
Charles I, King 145
Charles, Prince of Wales 24
Chrétien, Jean 7
Clark, Joseph (Joe) 140
Clarkson, Adrienne 8; controversy for not attending Lois Hole's Memorial Service, 249-250; explains role of Governor General with respect to foreign trips 10; visits Edmonton, 166
Coleman, Jim 226
Connaught, Duke of 25
Consular Ball 227-228

Davies, Edward (Red) 5
Dawson, Peter 174
Dent, Ivor 178
Desrochers, Louis 216-217
Diefenbaker, John 3
Doakes, Joan 232
Dufferin, Lord 11
Duke of Edinburgh Awards 222

Edward VIII, King unveils Vimy Ridge Memorial 6-7; visits Calgary 1919, 72; 213
Edward, Prince, Earl of Wessex attended Commonwealth Games 1978, 5; 164
Egbert, Eva 52, 57; 188
Egbert, William accepts Greenfield's resignation 95; at Government House,

52,56,58,60; bio. 123-124; installation, 123-124, 125; New Years' Levee, 188

Elizabeth II, Queen of Canada (as Princess visited Alberta, 160); attends Juno Beech ceremonies, 7; celebration of official birthday in Canada, 200; Golden Jubilee Celebrations, 201-204; Head of the Order of St John of Jerusalem, 77; role of Monarch, 2-9; unveils memorial honouring Canada's role in WWI and WWII, 7; 8;17; 23-24; 146; visits Alberta, 161, 162

Elizabeth, The Queen Mother visit to Edmonton in 1939, 65, 158; visit to Edmonton in 1985, 163

Elzinga, Peter 103

Ferguson, John installed as Chancellor of the University of Alberta, 85

Fraser, Catherine 17; 250

George VI, King 3; gave Royal Assent 110; Letters Patent of 1947, 9; visit to Edmonton in 1939, 65, 158

Getty, Don 153; 157; 170

Gouin, Lomer 16

Government House 51-63; closure of 63

Governors General role of, 9-10; 14

Great Seal of Alberta 37-39

Greenfield, Herbert 95

Grey, Earl 121; 228

Griesbach, William "Billy" 130

Gun Salutes 40-41; 149

Harvey, Horace 15-18; 122; 123

Hole, Lois 20; administers oath to new Chancellor of the University of Alberta, 85; admitted as Dame of the Venerable Order of St John of Jerusalem, 80-81; bio. 141;death, 249; hospital named in her honour, 249; installation, 141-144; Memorial Service, 249; New Years' Levee, 28, 29, 49, 198-199; poppy campaign ceremony, 210; presents Order of St. John Life Saving Medal, 221; Speech from the Throne, 150, 153, 164, 178; stretches constitutional practice, 106-109; themes pursued during her term of office, 119-121; transportation difficulties, 74; wears formal gown, 49; visit to sovereign, 22-23; 24; Victoria Day Celebrations, 200-204; 237-238;247; views on health care, 249

Hole, Ted 221

Hugill, John 101

Hunley, Helen admitted as Dame of the Order of St John of Jerusalem, 80; bio. 138; 139; installation as Lieutenant-Governor, 39, 135; New Years' Levee, 193-194; opens McDougall Centre, 70; Remembrance Day, 215; Speech from the Throne, 153; swears in MLA, 156; unveils portrait, 170; visit to sovereign, 22; wears robe-of-office, 48-49

Jeffers, Allan architect of Government House, 51

Johns, Walter 191

King, William Lyon Mackenzie 16; attempts to bring peace between Bowen and Aberhart, 63, 100, 112, 159-160; 124, 125;

Klein, Ralph 103-105; relationship with Lois Hole, 106-109; sworn in as Premier, 157; tears down 58 St. George's Crescent residence, 68,70; 143;153;156;178; 250

Kerr, Illingworth 168

Kerr, William A.R. 189

Kowalski, Ken 103-104; 115

Kozar, Frank 199

Kuhse, Captain George 249

Kwong, His Honour Norman bio. 251; installation, 250-251;installation speech, 251;no official residence, 252

Langland, George 73

Laskin, Bora 110-111

Lassandro, Florence 125

Laurier, Wilfrid 94; 122

Lieutenant-Governor's Badge 44,45,48

Lieutenant-Governor's Cup 228-231

Lieutenant-Governor's Flag (Standard) 42-45

Lieutenant-Governor's office 64
Lieutenant-Governor's residence 50; (58 St. George's Crescent) 68-70;
Lieutenant-Governor, role of 10-14
Lieutenant-Governor's uniform 45
Lougheed, Jeanne 66
Lougheed, Peter 45; becomes Premier, 98; 102; institutes Albera Order of Excellence, 75; restores Government House, 65-66; view of Grant MacEwan, 104;113;134;151;178;192
Low, Solon 97; 112-113
Lynch, Donna first female aide-de-camp 30
Lynch-Staunton 24; accepts new Lieutenant-Governor's flag, 42; first Chancellor of the Alberta Order of Excellence, 76; relationship with Peter Lougheed, 102; viewpoint about residence at 58 St. George's Crescent, 68; visit to sovereign, 21-22;

MacEwan, Grant 23;28; 121; bio. 132-135; Canadian Derby, 226-227; death, 178; installation, 135-136; New Years' Levee, 191-192, 193, 216; presides over the swearing in ceremony of Peter Lougheed as Premier, 98; 104; proclaims the official flag of Alberta, 114; requires a residence, 67, 79; Speech from the Throne, 151-152, 161-162; State Funeral, 176-178; unveiling portrait, 168-169; wears the traditional "Windsor" uniform, 45;
MacIntosh, Irwin 21
MacLennan, Dan 250
Manning, Ernest becomes Premier, 97; embarrassed because of lack of residence for the Lieutenant-Governor, 67; receives Order of Excellence, 76; 132;133;189;191;216
Margaret, Princess visits Edmonton, 163;224
Marskell, James chauffeur of Lieutenant-Governor, 73
McCarthy, D'Alton 125
McClung, John "Buzz" 17; 19; 154-155
Mckinnon, James 66
Meighen, Arthur 125
Mills, Edith 233
Milner, Stanley A. 216
Mitchell, Grant 156

Michener, Roland 9; begins regular meetings with Lieutenant-Governors, 27-28
Monarch, role of 2-9; 14
Moore, Kenneth 135
Mowat, Oliver 11
Mulroney, Brian 3; 140

New Years' Levee origins, 187
Newby, Captain H. S. 174
Notley, Grant 106

O'Connor, George 17; 130
Oliver, Frank Edmonton home serves as first residence of the Lieutenant-Governor, 50-51; Government House, 51; receives honourary degree, 83; 94
Olson, Horace "Bud" admitted to Venerable Order of St John of Jerusalem, 78; bio. 140-141; chats with Towers and Klein, 105; conflict with Gordon Towers, 195-198, 215-216; death, 178; hosts function in Legislative office of the Lieutenant-Governor, 64; installation, 140; lowers flag at death of Diana, Princess of Wales, 43; meets school children,234-235, 236-237; moves location of New Years' Levee, 28, 195-197; poppy campaign ceremony, 207-208; presides over investiture of the Order of St John of Jerusalem, 220; receives honourary degree from the University of Alberta, 82; Speech from the Throne, 152, 164; unveils portrait, 171; wears morning suit, 47;
Olson, Lucille 234-235
Order of Excellence 75-77
Order of St John of Jerusalem 77-81
Osborn, Dr. Andrew 174

Page, Percy 17; bio. 132; death, 178; lived in his own home, 67; installation, 132-133; 161; invested as Knight of Grace of the Order of St John of Jerusalem, 79; New Years' Levee, 190-191, 196; official car, 72; portrait unveiling, 167
Pearson, Lester B. 5
Petty, Louise 190-191
Philip, Prince, Duke of Edinburgh attended

Commonwealth Games 1978, 4-5; Duke of Edinburgh Awards, 222; 160-161
Picarielle, Emilio 125
Poppy Campaign 206-210
Primrose, Lily New Years' Levee, 188-189
Primrose, Philip 15;17;81;100; installation, 129; State Funeral, 173-175
Privy Seal 38

Queen's Counsel 218-219

Reid, Gavin becomes Premier, 96; 188
Remembrance Day origins, 205-206; ceremony 211-216
Robertson, Gerald Q.C. 219
Royal Assent 110-113
Rule, John architect of residence at 58 St. George's Crescent, 67
Rutherford, Alexander 94

Sauvé, Jeanne 80; 166
Savage, A.H. 223
Schreyer, Edward 10
Sifton, Arthur 94
Simons, Paula comments on Lois Hole's constitutional elasticity, 108; view of demolition of residence at 58 St. George's Crescent, 68
Sophie, Countess of Wessex 164
Spaghetti Tree 233
Speech from the Throne ceremony of, iv-v; 145-154
Smith, Bruce 17; 132; 134
Steinhauer, Ralph appears to veer from constitutional practice, 106; bio. 134-135; installation, 134; New Years' Levee, 192-193; ponders Royal Assent, 113; portrait unveiled, 168; presents Alberta Lifesaving Award, 223; Remembrance Day, 214; transportation difficulties, 73-74; 79; wore Chief's regalia, 45-46; visit to sovereign, 21
Stinson, Shirley, 216

Tackaberry, Foss 201
Taylor, Gordon sworn into cabinet, 155-156
Towers, Doris 147

Towers, Gordon 17; bio. 140; conflict with "Bud" Olson, 195-198, 215-216; conflict with Kowalski, 115; death, 178; installation, 138-140; 147; 154; New Years' Levee, 193,195; portrait unveiled, 171; relations with Ralph Klein, 103-105, 156-157; swearing in of Premier Klein, 157; theme for his term as Lieutenant-Governor, 121; wore morning suit, 47; 79;
Tory, Annie 57
Trudeau, Pierre Elliott 6
Tweedsmuir, Lord 60; cenotaph unveiling, 212
Tyrrell, Dr. Lorne recipient of the Order of Excellence, 217-218

Vanek, Anthony appeals to "Visitor" of the University of Alberta for redress of grievance, 84-85
Vanier, Georges P. 79
Vice-regal Gun Salute 40-41
Vice-regal Salute 40
Visitor, position of the University of Alberta 82-84

Wakefield, Keith 196
Wallace, Robert C. 188
Walsh, Bertha 126; 128
Walsh, William 26; accepts Reid as Premier, 96; accepts Aberhart as Premier, 97; bio. 125-126; installation, 126-128, 129; New Years' Levee, 188 refused monies to refurbish Government House, 60; 77; relationship with Ministers of his government, 99; "Visitor" to the University of Alberta, 83;
Weston, Hillary 12
Wilkinson, Neil 144
Willingdon, Lord 9
Winspear, Francis, G. 216

ISBN 1-41205317-X